Dates and Meanings of Religious and Other Festivals

With a calendar for 1989–1993

John G. Walshe M.A., Dip RE. Ph.D.

W. FOULSHAM & CO. LIMITED
LONDON • NEW YORK • TORONTO • CAPE TOWN • SYDNEY

W. Foulsham & Co. Limited
Yeovil Road, Slough, Berks., England

ISBN 0–57201514–3

Printed in Great Britain
at The Bath Press, Avon

Contents

Acknowledgements

Thanks are due to the following for assistance and contributions.

Manjeet Arri

John Cunningham

Manju Dhillon

John Gaus

Boris Lazarev

David Osen

Ian Potts

Gurdev Pujara

Omparkash Sharma

G. U. Syed

Vivien Roe

Sham Sunder Lal Val

Astrology Dept., Tibetan Medical Institue, Dharamsala

Rev. Bandula

and to Dr. Shrikala Warrier for constant research support and original material.

Preface

An expanding tapestry of religious and secular festivals is being woven into our events calendar. In addition to the official philosophical or theological weave and signature there are strong local identifying dashes of dye that give emphases to specific community celebrations. The creative tensions between the orthodoxy of the official "custodians of the faith" and the dynamism of the doers require sensitive interpretation. There are aspects to particular celebrations that are social, psychological, chauvinistic and even competitive as well as theological or philosophical. This book is, in the main, an explanation by individuals of what and why they celebrate. It retains the enthusiasm of the committed. It has evolved over seven years as a channelled response to teachers, nurses, doctors, solicitors, police officers, social workers and others who enquired in specific or general terms about the celebrations in the community in which they worked. In the past most enquiries related to festivals that were imminent, current or past. Nowadays many enquiries relate to the dating of future festivals that are still one or two years away.

The dating of some future festivals requires considerable effort and skill. Sources in Britain and on the Sub-continent have been consulted. Agreement is not easily arrived at. All dates should be checked locally as close in time to the festival as possible. The medium is often the message. The effort to ascertain dates has for some of us been the opening of religio-cultural doors that have revealed a variety of transcultural treasures to be shared.

Calendars

The calendar is a method of adjusting the natural divisions of time with respect to each other for both administrative purposes and for the observance of religious festivals. The term 'calendars' derived from the Latin word 'kalendae' which designated the first day of the month in Roman times.

Celestial bodies provide the basic standard for determining the calendar. The basic calendar units are the day, month and year, derived from the movements of the earth, the moon and the sun respectively.

A Day

A Day is measured by the rotation of the earth on its axis. The duration of one complete rotation with respect to the stars is called the sidereal day (from the Latin 'sidus' which means 'star') a unit of time that is important in astronomy.

The cycle of night and day has considerable bearing on man's life. Hence, the solar day, or the interval between two passages of the sun across the meridian, is the basis of the civil calendar. The solar day is longer than the sidereal day by approximately four minutes.

A Month

A lunar month is the time it takes the moon to complete a cycle of phases. It has an average length of 29.5 days.

A Year

A year corresponds to the cycle of the seasons and is the result of the sun's apparent movement through the constellations of the zodiac as the earth moves around the sun.

The astronomical year is defined as the movement of the sun over the earth's hemisphere. The instant when the centre of the sun's disk crosses the equator is known as the vernal equinox, and the time interval between two vernal equinoxes is known as the seasonal or tropical year. A year averages 365 days.

A Week

The week is a calendar unit that is almost universally used. It is an artificial unit of time, although its length of seven days relates it to the phases of the moon. The Hebrews were the first to use it. In most languages the days of the week are named after the seven moving celestial objects that were known in ancient times, namely the Sun, Moon, Mars, Mercury, Jupiter, Venus and Saturn.

Types of Calendars

There are three basic types of calendars: the lunar, lunisolar and solar, based on the phases of the moon and the apparent movements of the sun.

Lunar Calendar

The oldest kind of calendar is the lunar calendar. In this type, the civil month is approximately the same length as the actual lunar month, and the first day of each civil month coincides with the new moon.

To establish agreement between the civil month, composed of a whole number of days, and the lunar month of 29.5306 days, an early solution was to have civil months that were alternately 29 and 30 days long. This made for an average civil month of 29.5 days – a lag of 0.0306 days behind the actual lunar month. Later lunar calendars grouped twelve civil months in a lunar year of 365 days. The year therefore lagged behind the cycle of the moon's phases by 0.3672 days. One way of compensating fairly precisely for this lag was to insert one day in the calendar (intercalate) every three years. Alternative solutions were to intercalate three days over a period of eight years, seven days in nineteen years, or eleven days in thirty years.

Lunisolar Calendars

Once the significance of the solar year of 365.25 days came to be recognised, an exact relationship was sought between the solar year and the lunar month. One of the first solutions was to add a month to every three years. Alternatively, if three months are added to eight lunar years or seven months to nineteen lunar years, the adjustment closely approximates eight or nineteen solar years respectively. Both the eight-year (Octennial) cycle and the nineteen-year (Metonic) cycle were used by the ancient Greeks. The Metonic cycle is fairly precise and is still used in ecclesiastical calendar calculations.

Solar Calendars

In modern times, the lunar month has been largely rejected in order to ensure better agreement between the civil month and the solar year. The twelve months are retained but are no longer lunar, so that the new moon may fall on any day of the month. Only the value of 365.2422 days as the average length of the year is fundamental to the establishment of the solar calendar.

A year of 365 days came to be used with an additional day intercalated every fourth year. The intercalary year was designated the leap year. This was the solution adopted in the Julian calendar. However, as the fraction to be compensated for is, in fact, 0.2422 days and not 0.25 days, an addition of one day every four years results in an excess of 0.0078 days per year and a cumulative error of about three days every four centuries. The Gregorian reforms which resulted in the modern Western calendar eliminates, to a large extent, this remaining discrepancy.

The Western Calendar

The Western calendar had its origin in the desire for a solar calendar that kept in step with the seasons and possessed fixed rules of intercalation. With the rise of Christianity, it also had to provide a method of dating movable religious feasts such as Easter which were based on lunar reckoning. To reconcile the lunar and solar schemes, features of the Roman Republican calendar and the Egyptian calendar were used.

The early Romans used a lunar calendar in which the lengths of the months alternated between 29 and 30 days. The civil year was composed of ten months and therefore of 295 days. The first month in the calendar was March. The seventh, eighth, ninth and tenth months were named September, October, November and December – Latin words indicating the position of these months in the year.

According to legend, it was around 700 BC that January and February were added as the eleventh and twelfth months of the year. February consisted of only 28 days.

In the course of time, the Roman Republican calendar became increasingly out of step with the seasons. A need therefore arose for a calendar that would allow the months to be based on phases of the moon and the year to be in line with the seasons.

The reformation of the Roman calendar was undertaken by Julius Caesar in 46 BC. The lunar calendar was abandoned. Instead the months were arranged on a seasonal basis and the solar year was used, with its length taken as 365¼ days.

It was also decided that the vernal equinox would fall on March 25. The civil year was fixed at 365 days and an additional day was intercalated every four years so that the solar year would remain in agreement with the seasons. The extra day was added after February 28.

The Julian reforms also reinstated January 1 as the first day of the year. January 45 BC thus inaugurates the Julian calendar. A discrepancy in names was retained, however, in that the months of September to December still had their former names, although they were now the ninth to the twelfth months of the year.

The Gregorian Calendar

The average length of the year in the Julian calendar, fixed at 365¼ days, is eleven minutes longer than the solar year. There was thus a cumulative error amounting to nearly eight days in the course of 1000 years, and the calendar once again became increasingly out of phase with the seasons.

In 1582, Pope Gregory XIII reformed the Julian calendar by shortening the year by ten days to bring the vernal equinox to March 21. It was further ordained that no centennial years should be leap years unless they were exactly divisible by 400. Thus, 1700, 1800 and 1900 were not leap years although the year 2000 will be. The reform measures also laid down the rules for calculating the date of Easter.

Easter was the most important feast of the Christian Church and its place in the calendar determined the position of the rest of the Church's movable feasts. Its timing depended on both the moon's phases and the vernal equinox. Church authorities therefore had to seek some way of reconciling the lunar and solar calendars.

Easter was primarily designated a spring festival, and the earliest Christians celebrated it at the same time as the Jewish Passover festival, that is during the night of the first full moon of the first month of spring (Nisan 14 and 15). By the middle of the second century, most Churches had transferred this celebration to the Sunday after the Passover feast. The Council of Nicea observed the feast on a Sunday. Yet many disparities remained in fixing the date of Easter. Today the Eastern Churches follow the Julian calendar and the Western Churches the Gregorian calendar, so that in some years there may be a month's difference in the times of celebration.

The Gregorian calendar was adopted exactly according to the mandate of the Pope in France, Spain, Portugal and Italy in 1582. The Protestant countries, however, were slow to adopt it. In England it was not adopted until 1752.

The Baha'i Calendar

Although the Baha'i faith is the youngest of the world's major religions, it has introduced its own calendar which it would like to see universally applied. The desire for a Baha'i calendar eminates from a concept of oneness, 'The earth is but one country, and mankind its citizens' (Baha'u'llah).

The Baha'i Era dates from 1844. Its calendar year consists of nineteen months, each of nineteen days duration, adding up to 361 days with four intercalary days included between the eighteenth and nineteenth months. The leap year has five intercalary days.

The names of the nineteen months represent attributes of God, and the avoidance of references to old pagan feasts or Roman names emphasises the arrival of a new era. The months are:

Splendour	March 3 (the New Year)–March 21
Beauty	March 22–April 28
Grandeur	April 29–May 17
Light	May 18–June 5
Mercy	June 6–June 24
Word	June 25–July 13
Perfection	July 13–August 1
Names	August 2–August 20
Might	August 21–September 8
Will	September 9–September 27
Knowledge	September 28–October 16
Power	October 17–November 4
Speech	November 5–November 23
Questions	November 24–December 12
Honour	December 13–December 31
Sovereignty	January 1–January 19
Dominion	January 20–February 7
Loftiness	February 8–March 2
Intercalary days	February 26–March 1

An additional intercalary day is included on February 29 in leap years.

The Baha'i days, corresponding to Saturday to Sunday are:

Glory	Justice
Beauty	Majesty
Perfection	Independence
Grace	

The day starts and ends at sunset (6.00 pm is fixed for polar regions) and celebrations therefore commence on the eve of the day before listed dates. New Year, for example, is ushered in after sunset on March 20.

On nine of the eleven annual holidays, adults refrain from work and children do not attend school. The nine days are:

The Festival of New Year	March 21
The Festival of the first day of Ridvan	April 21
The Festival of the ninth day of Ridvan	April 29
The Festival of the twelfth day of Ridvan	May 2
The Festival of the Declaration of the Bab	May 23 at 2 hours 11 minutes after sunset
The Commemoration of the Ascension of Baha'u'llah	May 29
The Commemoration of the Martyrdom of the Bab	July 9
The Celebration of the Birth of the Bab	October 20
The Celebration of the Birth of Baha'u'llah	November 12

Baha'i celebrations avoid the use of rituals.

The Buddhist Calendar

The Buddhist calendar is a lunar one usually consisting of twelve months, with the inclusion of an additional month every four or five years. 1988, for instance, had thirteen months.

The full moon days in each month are important to Buddhists and many of them are celebrated with colourful ceremonies. The full moon day in the month of Veshakha (Vaisakha) is particularly significant in Theravada Buddhist countries such as Sri Lanka and Thailand, as it commemorates the birth, enlightenment and death of the Buddha. Followers of the Mahayana and Zen traditions normally celebrate each of these events on separate days.

The Buddhist calendar tends to vary from one country to another, and from one school of Buddhism to another.

In Britain the three main schools in order of arrival are Theravada, Zen and Tibetan.

In Pali, the ancient North Indian language, the names of the Buddhist months are

Citta	Assayuja
Vefaka	Kattika
Jettha	Maggafira
Afalha	Pussa
Favana	Maga
Potthabada	Phagguna

The additional or thirteenth month is called Adhivefaka.

The Chinese Calendar

Evidence from the Shang oracle bone inscriptions show that as early as the fourteenth century BC, the Shang Chinese had established the solar year at 365¼ days and lunations (the time between new moons) at 29½ days. The ancient Chinese calendar was lunisolar and the ordinary year contained twelve lunar months. As this was shorter than the solar year, in seven years out of every nineteen a thirteenth incalary month was inserted during the year to bring the calendar back in step with the seasons. Because of this, and the need for accurate dates for agriculture, there was also an underlying solar year which was divided into 24 sections. These have colourful names such as the Waking of Insects, Grain in the Ear and White Dew. Although most festivals are fixed by the lunar calendar some, such as Qingming, are fixed in the solar cycle.

The Chinese year begins with the first new moon after the sun enters Aquarius, that is the second new moon after the winter solstice. Thus New Year's Day falls any time between January 21 and February 20.

The years in the Chinese calendar are named after twelve animals which follow one another in rotation. According to one form of the legend, these animals quarrelled one day as to who was to head the cycle of years. When asked to decide, the gods suggested a contest. Whoever was to reach the bank of a certain river first would head the cycle, and the rest of the animals would be grouped accordingly. All the animals assembled at the river and the ox plunged in. Unknown to him, the rat jumped on his back. Just before the ox reached the bank, the rat jumped off his back and stepped ashore. Thus the cycle starts with the rat.

The animals in order, with their Chinese names and Western equivalent zodiacal signs, are:

Tzu	Rat	Aries
Chou	Ox	Taurus
Yin	Tiger	Gemini
Mau	Hare	Cancer
Chen	Dragon	Leo
Szu	Snake	Virgo
Wu	Horse	Libra
Wei	Ram	Scorpio
Sher	Monkey	Sagittarius
Yu	Rooster	Capricorn
Hsii	Dog	Aquarius
Hai	Bear	Pisces

Chinese horoscopes are based on the characteristics of the animal sign of the year of a person's birth, rather than the month as for Western horoscopes. Every Chinese knows their animal sign, and from it one can easily guess their age (to a multiple of twelve years).

Nowadays in China and Hong Kong the Western calendar is used for all administrative purposes, but the lunar calendar is still popularly used for most festivals, religious activities and birthdays.

The Hindu Calendar

While the Republic of India has adopted the Gregorian calendar for secular purposes, the religious life of Hindus continues to be governed by the traditional Hindu calendar, which is based primarily on the lunar cycle but adapted to solar reckoning.

The oldest form of the Hindu calendar is known from texts of about 1000 BC. It divides a solar year of approximately 360 days into twelve lunar months. In order to align it with the solar year of 365 days, a leap month was intercalated every 60 months.

The year was divided into three thirds of four months, each of which would be introduced by a special religious rite, the 'Chaturmasya' (four-month rite). Each of these periods was further divided into two parts (seasons or 'rtu'):

Spring	Vasantha	Mid-February to mid-April
Summer	Grishma	Mid-April to mid-June
Rainy Season	Varsa	Mid-June to mid-August
Autumn	Sarad	Mid-August to mid-October
Winter	Hemanta	Mid-October to mid-December
Dewy Season	Sisira	Mid-December to mid-February

The month, counted from full moon to full moon, was divided into two halves (paksha) of waning (krsna paksha) and waxing (suklapaksha and special rituals were prescribed on the days of the new moon (amavasya) and full moon (purnima). The lunar day (tithi), a thirtieth part of the lunar month, was reckoned to be the basic unit of the calendar. However, as the lunar month is only about 29½ solar days, the tithi does not correspond with the natural day of 24 hours.

The 'Jyotisa-Vedanga', a treatise on time reckoning dated around 100 BC, adds a larger unit of five years (yuga) to these divisions. A further distinction was made between the uttarayana (northern course), when the sun rises every morning farther north, and dakshinayana (southern course), when it rises progressively south.

The reckoning, in general, was mostly dictated by the requirements of rituals, the time of which had to be fixed correctly. When astrology came into vogue for casting horoscopes and making predictions, zodiacal time measurement was introduced into the calendar.

The year began with the entry of the sun (sankranti) in the sign of Aries. The names of the zodiacal signs (rasi) were taken over and translated into Sanskrit. The table below indicates the zodiacal signs in the Hindu calendar and their Western equivalents.

Mesa	Ram	Aries
Vrsabha	Bull	Taurus
Mithura	Twins	Gemini
Karkata	Crab	Cancer
Simha	Lion	Leo
Kanya	Maiden	Virgo
Tula	Scale	Libra
Vrschika	Scorpion	Scorpio

Dhanus	Bow	Sagittarius
Makara	Crocodile	Capricorn
Kumbha	Water jar	Aquarius
Mina	Fish	Pisces

While the solar system has significance for astrology, time for ritual purposes continues to be reckoned by the lunar calendar. The names of the months in this system are as follows:

Chaitra	March–April
Vaisakha	April–May
Jyaistha	May–June
Ashada	June–July
Sravana	July–August
Bhadrapada	August–September
Asvina	September–October
Karthika	October–November
Margasirsa	November–December
Pausa	December–January
Magha	January–February
Phalguna	February–March

In the course of time, India also adopted the seven-day week (saptaha) from the West and the days were named after the corresponding planets.

Sunday	Ravivara	Sun
Monday	Somavara	Moon
Tuesday	Mangalvara	Mars
Wednesday	Budhvara	Mercury
Thursday	Brihspativara	Jupiter
Friday	Sukravara	Venus
Saturday	Sanivara	Saturn

The Eras

Not before the first century BC is there any evidence that the years of events were recorded in well-defined eras.

Among those that have remained influential are the Vikrama Era (begun in 58 BC), the Saka Era (which commenced from AD 78), the Gupta Era (commenced from AD 320) and the Harsha Era (which began from AD 606). All these were dated from some significant historical event, though the first two are the most commonly used.

In the Hindu calendar, the date of an event takes the following form: month, fortnight (either waxing or waning moon), name (usually the number) of the tithi in that fortnight and the year of the particular era which the writer follows.

Important Hindu festivals are usually based on the lunar calendar. However, the sun's entry into the sign of Aries, marking the beginning of the astrological year, and the sun's entry into the sign of Capricorn (makara sankranti), marking the winter solstice, are also regarded as important days in the calendar. The latter coincides with a harvest festival, which in the southern Indian state of Tamil Nadu is widely celebrated as the Pongal Festival.

The Jewish Calendar

The Jewish calendar in use today is lunisolar, the years being solar and the month lunar. The year consists of twelve months which are alternately 29 and 30 days in length. In order to celebrate the festivals in their proper season, the difference between the lunar year (354 days) and the solar year (365½ days) is made up by intercalating a thirteenth month of 30 days in the third, sixth, eighth, eleventh, fourteenth, seventeenth and nineteenth year of a nineteen-year cycle. The month so added is called Adar Sheni (second Adar) and the year, a leap year. The intercalary year can contain 383, 384 or 385 days, while ordinary years contain 353, 354 or 355 days.

The year commences at the new moon of Tishri (September to October) but its beginning may be shifted by a day for various reasons, among them the rule that the Day of Atonement must not fall on a Friday or Sunday, the seventh day of Tabernacles or a sabbath.

The months are counted (following the biblical custom) from Nisan. Only a few biblical month names are known. The present ones are of Babylonian origin.

The Jewish Era in use today is dated from the supposed year of the creation, calculated on biblical data to coincide with 3761 BC. In giving Hebrew dates, it is customary to use Hebrew letters for numbers and to omit the thousands from the year number.

The Hebrews can be considered to have established the week as a unit of time. The pivot of the week is the sabbath, or day of rest, which corresponds to Saturday in the modern calendar.

For practical purposes, for example, for reckoning the commencement of the sabbath, the day begins at sunset. The calendar day of 24 hours, however, always begins at 6 pm.

The names of the months in the Hebrew calendar and the number of days in each are listed below.

Hebrew Name	Babylonian Name	Length
1. Nisan	Nisannu	30 days
2. Iyyar	Ayaru	29 days
3. Sivan	Simanu	30 days
4. Tammuz	Du'uzu	29 days
5. Av	Abu	30 days
6. Ellul	Ululu	29 days
7. Tishri	Tashretu	30 days

17

8. Marheshvan (Heshvan)	Arakshanana	29/30 days
9. Kislev	Kishnuu	29/30 days
10. Tevet	Tabetu	29/30 days
11. Shevat	Shabatu	30 days
12. Adae	Addaru	29 days
		(30 days in leap year)

The Muslim Calendar

The Muslim Era is computed from the year of the Hegira (AD 622) or the migration of the Prophet Mohammed and his followers from Mecca to Medina. The second caliph, Omar I, who reigned from AD 634–644, set the first day of the month Muharram as the beginning of the year.

The year in the Muslim calendar is lunar and always consists of twelve lunar months alternating 30 and 29 days long, beginning with the approximate new moon. The year has 354 days, but the last month, Dhu-al-hijjah (Zul-Hijja), sometimes has an intercalated day, bringing it up to 30 days and making a total of 355 days for that year. The months do not keep to the same seasons in relation to the sun because there are no intercalations of months.

Ramadhan, the ninth month of the Muslim calendar, is observed throughout the Muslim world as a period of fasting. According to the Quran, Muslims must see the new moon with the naked eye before they can begin their fast. Should the new moon prove to be invisible, then the month Shaban immediately preceding Ramadhan, will be reckoned as 30 days in length and the fast will commence on the day following the last day of Shaban.

Though the Christian Era may be in official use, people in Muslim countries continue to use the Muslim Era for non-official purposes. Some Islamic countries have made a compromise on this matter. As early as AD 1677, Turkey took over the solar (Julian) year with its month names, but kept the Muslim Era. March 1 was fixed as the beginning of the year. Late in the nineteenth century, the Gregorian calendar was adopted. In the twentieth century, President Ataturk, along with other major reforms, ordered a complete change to the Christian Era.

Iran, under Reza Shah Pahlavi (1925–41), also adopted the solar year, but retained the Persian names for the months and the Muslim Era. March 21 is the beginning of the Iranian year.

The names of the months in the Muslim calendar and the number of days in each are listed below.

Name	Length
1. Muharram	30 days
2. Safar	29 days
3. Rabee Ul-Awwal	30 days
4. Rabee Ul-Thani	29 days

5. Jumadi Ul-Awwal	30 days
6. Jumadi Ul-Thani	29 days
7. Rajab	30 days
8. Shaban	29 days
9. Ramadhan	30 days
10. Shawwal	29 days
11. Zul-Qeda	30 days
12. Zul-Hijja	29 days

Muslim Festivals

Feasts and festivals have become an integral part of human life in almost every society these days. In most cases, their origin can be traced to ancient social rites, religious practices or anniversaries of memorable events. For Muslims, all religious festivals have special significance. In fact, at the end of different modes of worship, Islam has instituted a kind of festival. The festival following the daily prayers of the week is the Friday Prayer, called Juma Prayer, the one following the month of fasting is called Eid-ul-Fitr, while the festival following the ceremony of Haj is known as Eid-ul-Adha.

These festivals are not merely the moment of joy and happiness. They are also a form of worship in themselves, as Islam grafts the remembrance of God with every activity of a Muslim. It has woven each action of the believer with God's remembrance so that even the ordinary activities of life, like sitting, walking, sleeping, wearing shoes or garments, going in or out of the house, going on a journey or returning from it, selling or buying something, eating, drinking, washing, bathing, entering or leaving a mosque, meeting a friend or facing an enemy, seeing the moon, starting any work or finishing it, even sneezing, yawning or taking medicine, have been closely attached to his remembrance.

No wonder the idol worshippers of Mecca labelled the Holy Prophet as one who had gone crazy about God. A worldly person would regard these things as sheer madness, but the man who has understood the reality of life knows that the true purpose of life lies in his devotion and remembrance of God Almighty. Therefore the day of a festival for a Muslim is not merely a day of fasting and merry-making, but is also spent in praising Allah, remembering his attributes, and thanking him for his countless bounties.

Islam is a religion of moderation, therefore it forbids its followers to indulge in extravagance at any time. It does not allow them to go to extremes so as to stand on the brink of insanity either with joy or with grief and sorrow. It teaches them to eat what God has provided for them but to be moderate. The Holy Quran states:

'O' mankind eat of that which is lawful and wholesome in the earth; and do not follow in the footsteps of Satan; surely he is your declared enemy.' (2.169)

Islam also instructs its followers to share their happiness with others, especially the needy and the poor. As regards the consumption of food, Muslims are asked not to waste any food. The Holy Quran states:

'Children of Adam, put your minds and bodies in a state of tidiness at every time and place of worship and eat and drink but be not wasteful; surely, he does not love the wasteful.' (7.32).

It is important to note that as Islamic festivals are based on lunar sightings rather than lunar reckonings, it is not possible to make exact forecasts of the dates.

The Eastern Orthodox Church

In 1054 a split occured between the four Eastern patriarchates and the Roman (Western) patriarchate. The Orthodox Eastern Church, also known as the Orthodox Church and the Greek Orthodox Church, is the federation of thirteen autocephalous (meaning 'having its own head') Orthodox Churches chiefly in Greece, Rumania, Bulgaria, Yuguslavia, Cyprus, the USSR and the Middle East. Together they comprise about one-sixth of the world's Christian population.

Serbian Orthodox Church

The full title of the Serbian Orthodox Church is 'The Serbian Holy Eastern Orthodox Ecumenic and Apostolic Church'.

Although it is an independent autonomous church in administrative matters, the Serbian Orthodox Church is in full spiritual communion with all other Orthodox Churches.

Up to the thirteenth century, the Serbian Christian population was under the jurisdiction of the Greek Archibishop of Ochrid as well as under the jurisdiction of the few Latin dioceses (bishoprics) in the western part of the Balkans.

In 1219, St Sava achieved the unification and administrative organisation of the Serbs into the autocephalous Serbian Orthodox Archbishopric.

In 1766, the Turkish Sultan (Serbia was at that time under Turkish rule) abolished the Serbian patriarchate and subjected its territories to the jurisdiction of the patriarchate of Constantinople.

The Orthodox Church of Serbia proper began its separation from Constantinople in 1815, and in 1879 gained its full independence.

In 1920, after the First World War, all the autonomous Serbian Orthodox Churches amalgamated into one Serbian Orthodox Church which was simultaneously elevated to the rank of patriarchate.

Veneration of Patron Saints (Slava)

In the Serbian Orthodox Church there is a unique religious custom – not found in any other Orthodox Church – the veneration of patron saints by individual families. Every Serbian Orthodox family has its own patron saint, who is regarded as its special intercessor with God.

The tradition is that in the olden days the Serbian converts to Christianity selected as their patrons the saints on whose calendar days they were baptised. The honouring of the patron saints is regarded among the Serbs as a sacred national tradition. In the course of time a family might change its name, but the patron saint remains the same. His Feast Day is celebrated at home with an elaborate ceremonial and feasting which equals that of Pascha (Easter) and Christmas (Nativity) to Christ.

The Orthodox Church Calendar

The Orthodox Church still uses the Julian calendar as per the reform of Julius Caesar in 46 BC. The later calendar reform by Pope Gregory XIII in 1582 was rejected by the Orthodox Church who viewed the papal reform as divisive and lacking in due respect for the traditions and oneness of the Church. The enforcement of the Gregorian calendar by several temporal rulers was regarded without enthusiasm.

Today, the Orthodox Church in its adherence to the Julian calendar remains thirteen days behind other Christians in its determination of festival dates. As examples, Orthodox Christmas falls on January 7 and New Year's day falls on January 14 in the Gregorian calendar.

Celebrations Through the Year

This section is a calendar of celebrations and festivals from a variety of the world's religions and cultures. The origin of the festival is indicated after the date according to these abbreviations.

B	Baha'i	H	Hindu	S	Sikh
Bd	Buddhist	J	Japanese	Sec	Secular
C	Christian	Jw	Jewish	SL	Sri Lankan
CH	Chinese	M	Muslim	T	Tibetan
GB	Great Britain	O	Orthodox	Th	Thai

January
New Year's Day (C)

Celebrated both as a popular festival and holiday, and by the Church. January 1 is traditionally seen as a time for fresh starts and opportunities. 'A Happy New Year' is a greeting understood by everyone.

The feast of the Circumcision is also on this date, remembering the circumcision of Christ, as is the Jewish custom, eight days after birth.

Ganjitsu – Japanese New Year (J)

New Year's Day is celebrated with a morning visit to a shrine or temple. A family dinner the Osechi, is eaten. This is cooked on new year's eve and placed in the jyubaker or special box. Included with the dinner is a traditional Japanese rice cake containing Omochi and Zoni.

An ancient game, called hajoita, is played for Japanese pennies. The bats used for the game have colourful paintings on one side.

Parents 'spoil' their children a little on this day with cash gifts or otoshidama.

Epiphany (C)

This festival, twelve days after Christmas, was originally associated with the baptism of Christ, and was one of the main festivals of the early Christians.

In the West it celebrates the manifestation of Christ to the gentiles in the story of the wise men or 'magi'. They brought presents of gold for a king, frankincense for a priest and myrrh for the suffering he would endure. These gifts are presented at the altar in St James's Palace, Chapel Royal by the British royal family. This has been done for the last 700 years.

Customs for the Serbian Orthodox Christmas (O)

In commemoration of the nativity of the Son of God, our Lord Jesus Christ, Serbian people have a variety of significant and moving customs.

Badnjak – the yule log – is the first of a chain of many customs. The badnjak is a young oak tree which reminds us of the tree with which the righteous Joseph started the fire in the manger. When the Son of God was born, the badnjak is brought home, placed on the fire and burned on Christmas Eve. At the same time, straw is spread on the floor, and after prayers a lengthy supper is served.

Bringing the badnjak into the house represents Christ's entry into the world, into our home and into our hearts and souls.

The first visitor to the home early on Christmas morning is called Polaznik. With the branch from badnjak, he stirs up the fire, thus creating many sparks and wishing God's richest blessing to the family. He represents the shepherds who received the honour of being the first to see and announce the birth of our Saviour.

'Chesnica' is a simple bread or nut pastry. It is prepared on Christmas Day with a silver or gold coin baked into it. At dinner time it is broken, and a person receiving the piece of chesnica containing the coin is supposed to have good luck in the coming year. Chesnica represents the grace of God given to the Church by the Lord Jesus Christ for our salvation.

Customs are crowned with going to church for the Divine Liturgy and returning home with prayers, and singing hymns during the entire celebration.

Lohri and Maghi (S)

Lohri is the winter festival of Punjab, celebrated on the last day of the month of Poh in the Vikram or Hindu calendar. The night of Lohri is considered to be the coldest night of winter. A bonfire is lit in open country yards to keep out the cold. For many days before this festival, children go round people's houses singing folk songs and asking for Lohri. It is very similar to carol singing before Christmas, and similarly they are given money and sometimes special items of food.

Lohri is especially important for families with a newly-born baby or a newly-married son. Dried fruit, nuts, sultanas, sesame snaps, sweets, popcorn and rice flakes are eaten and distributed amongst relatives, friends and neighbours. Rice flakes, sesame seeds, popcorn and sesame sweets are also thrown in the bonfire for good luck. A young bride is encouraged to throw black sesame seeds (which are rare) in the fire because there is a saying that she will have as many sons as the black sesame seeds she throws in the fire.

Maghi is celebrated the next morning. It is the beginning of the new month and the Sikhs go to the nearby Gurdwara (Sikh Temple) to listen to the service for celebration of the new month. There is a big fair in the town of Muktsar in Punjab in memory of the tenth Guru of the Sikhs and the forty Sikh martyrs of Muktsar.

Makar Sankranti (H)

Makar Sankranti is observed by Hindus all over India as the Winter Solstice Festival. The day is spent in prayer and in Maharashtra, a special sweet made of sesame seeds (symbolising life) is distributed to friends and relatives.

Pongal (H)

Hindus in the southern Indian states of Tamil Nadu, Andhra Pradesh and Karnataka celebrate the Pongal-Sankranti festival to coincide with the winter solstice or the sun's entry into the sign of Capricorn. It is an important harvest festival and the celebrations extend over three days.

The first day is called Bhogi Pongal and is observed as a family feast. The main feature of the second day's celebrations is the worship of Surya or the sun god. The third day, Mathu Pongal, is the most important and is observed as the day for the worship of cattle. Cows and oxen are bathed and decorated with garlands of flowers and worshipped. Pongal, a sweet made of rice, is offered to the household deity and then distributed to family members as well as given to the cattle to eat.

Week of Prayer for Christian Unity (C)

Special services are held in which different denominations visit each others' churches, and pulpits are shared by visiting preachers. The weak of prayer is timed to end on January 25, the day on which the conversion of St Paul is remembered.

Basant Panchami (S)

Basant Panchami is the festival heralding the arrival of spring. It falls on the fifth day after Magh in the Vikram calendar. Fields turn yellow with mustard flowers and people dress themselves in yellow clothes. The Namdhari Sikhs celebrate this day as the birthday of their founder Guru Ram Singh Ji.

Vasanta Panchami (H)

The festival of Vasanta Panchami is enthusiastically celebrated by all Hindus in the month of Magha (January-February), mainly in honour of Sarasvati, the goddess of learning, wisdom and fine arts.

Sarasvati is an exceptionally charming goddess who plays on the musical instrument 'vina'. Her mount is a white swan. In every part of India, Hindu children start their education by writing the alphabet in front of the image of Sarasvati. She bestows every success on her worshippers, and without her grace none can attain proficiency in poetry, music or fine arts. Sarasvati is mainly a deity for personal worship and not community adoration. The worship of Sarasvati is particularly popular in Bengal.

February
St Brigid's Day (C)

This in Celtic tradition is the first day of spring. Rebirth was associated with Brigantia, the fertility goddess.

In Christian tradition St Brigid (or Bridget), a secondary patron saint of Ireland, is said to have been inspired by the teaching of St Patrick and to have established the first community of nuns in Kildare, an area which is now well known for its racehorses.

Candlemas – Feast of the Purification (C)

This festival celebrates the presentation of Christ in the Temple in Jerusalem 40 days after his birth, as the Jewish custom, and the purification ceremony of the Virgin Mary at the same time.

The English name 'Candlemas' refers to the custom of blessing and distributing candles and carrying them in procession before the mass. The light of the candles is symbolic of Christ as the light of the world.

Maghapuja or Dharma Day (Bd)

This festival, also called All Saints' Day, commemorates three events in the Buddha's life, namely the occasion when he took his two chief disciples, the occasion when he recited the rules by which monks should live, and his announcement that he would die in three month's time.

It is usually celebrated in a monastery in the presence of monks.

Setsubun – Japanese Spring Festival (J)

Special rituals are conducted to drive out evil spirits. A wooden rice measure containing beans is placed on the shrine by the head of the family household. As darkness falls, the beans are scattered around all the entrances of the house and in the dark corners. A small charm is then placed over each entrance to prevent the evil spirits from sneaking into the house.

Tu B'Shevat (Jw)

This marks the end of the heavy rain season in Israel and commemorates the New Year for Trees.

This minor festival has received new significance with the establishment of the modern state of Israel, where young children are encouraged to plant trees in celebration.

Jewish children may attend school on this day.

Nehar (J)

February 15 marks the 'Parinirvana' or death of the Buddha. In Soto Zen temples in Japan, all lights in the great meditation hall are put out. The entire congregation meditates and chants particular Buddhist scriptures, and finally the lamps are re-lit. This ritual expresses the hope that the teachings of the Buddha will endure for all time.

Shivrati (H)

The festival of Shivratri is celebrated by Hindus of all castes throughout India in the month of Phalguna (February–March). On this occasion people offer bilwa leaves to Shiva-linga (an iconic representation of Shiva) and spend the whole night in japa (prayer) and dhayana (meditation of Shiva). The ringing of bells is continued throughout the night. It lasts for fifteen days in Kashmir.

Shrove Tuesday (C)

'Shrove' is a term which is associated with confessing sins. The person is said to be shrove or shriven when they have confessed. It is thought necessary to confess sins before the solemnity of Lent. The day is just before Ash Wednesday which marks the beginning of Lent. The seriousness of Lent was preceded by merry-making, and people used up all the rich food in the house in preparation for a fast. Pancakes were a good way to use up food, and pancake races are a traditional sport.

The Mardi Gras carnival is now celebrated on an extravagant scale on this day.

Ash Wednesday

This marks the first day of Lent. In Roman Catholic churches, the previous year's palm crosses are burnt and the ashes sprinkled with holy water and then an ash cross marked on the participants as a sign of their penance. This is a reminder that sackcloth and ashes were a sign of penance in the Old Testament. Ash Wednesday is a day of fasting in the Catholic Church. As the minister signs each penitent he says, 'Remember man thou art but dust, and into dust you shall return'. This reminder of the mortality of man starts the preparation of prayer, penance and meditation for the great Easter festival.

Ash Wednesday commences the great liturgical cycle which culminated in the death and resurrection of Christ on Easter Sunday.

Lent (C)

Ash Wednesday to Holy Saturday – forty week days; Sundays are always festive. This period remembers the 40 days in the wilderness when Christ was tempted. Various degrees of fasting used to be practised but now people usually give up luxuries, give to others and spiritually prepare for Easter.

Chinese New Year (Ch)

New Year's Day is the most important event in the Chinese calendar and marks the beginning of the first lunar month. The festivities generally last for two or three weeks, though the first week tends to be the most important.

A week before the New Year, the family will honour the kitchen god, and he then reports to heaven on their conduct. While he is away the house must be thoroughly cleaned, debts should be paid, all food should be prepared, and the home decorated with flowers such as peach blossoms or jonquils. The kitchen god returns on New Year's Eve and fire crackers are let off.

For the New Year, people wear new clothes to represent the discarding of the old year and its misfortunes. Visits are made to relatives and friends with gifts of food and drink. Traditional foods include cakes made from rice flour or sesame seeds, and kumquats which signify prosperity. The usual greeting to be heard at New Year is, in Cantonese (the most widely spoken Chinese dialect in Britain), 'Kung hay fat choy' (pronounced like 'goong hay fut choy') meaning 'May you prosper'. Another important custom at this time is the giving of money in red paper packets by married couples to unmarried relatives, friends and children. In Cantonese these are called 'laisee' or 'hungpow' and are believed to bring luck.

The Lantern Festival on the first full moon of the New Year marks the end of the festivities. It celebrates the return of light, the coming of spring and the beginning of the growing season. Strings of lanterns of all shapes, sizes and colours are hung out to decorate homes and public places. Besides the family celebrations there are also colourful community events, of which the most important are the dragon and lion dances.

A lion dance can be seen at New Year in London's Chinatown. The 'two-man' pantomime lion dances through the streets to the sound of gongs and drums and reaches up to take money in red packets hung outside shops. It is believed that to give the lion money and food, such as kumquats and lettuce, will bring the establishment good fortune.

1989 is the year of the Snake.

Losar – The Tibetan New Year (T)

Losar is a three-day festival. On the first day, celebration are restricted mainly to the family. On the second and third days visits and gifts are exchanged with friends and relatives.

Houses are white-washed and thoroughly cleaned, people wear new clothes and special food is prepared. Good luck symbols such as dried ears of corn are placed in the house, and dishes of water and dough models called 'torna' are placed in household shrines along with other offerings.

People visit monasteries to make offerings and Buddhist monks conduct special religious ceremonies. A number of rituals are performed to drive away evil spirits and alms are given to the poor. There is also much merry-making with feasts, dancing and archery competitions.

1988 is designated as the year of the Earth Dragon, 2115 in the Tibetan Buddhist calendar.

Monlam Chenno – The Great Prayer Festival (T)

This follows the Tibetan New Year celebrations to ensure that all goes well in the coming year. It starts on the fourth day and goes on till the twenty-fifth day of the first month in the Tibetan calendar.

March
St David's Day (C)

St David is the patron saint of Wales and his feast day has been observed since the fourteenth century. Welsh people wear leeks or daffodils on this day. Very little is known about St David except that he lived in the far south-west of Wales, became an Archbishop and Primate of Wales and advised kings in Ireland.

Purim (Jw)

This marks the deliverance of the Jews of Persia from the persecution of Haman, the Prime Minister of King Ahaseurus, and his followers, who planned to exterminate them entirely throughout Persia and its Commonwealth, particularly because Haman hated the wise Jew Mordecai.

Providentially, the tables were turned on him when Mordecai's niece Esther was chosen by King Ahaseurus as his new queen. She pleaded for her people and saved them from destruction.

School may be attended, but the day is usually celebrated with much jollity, including fancy dress.

Hina Matsuri (J)

Hina Matsuri, or Dolls Festival, was originally celebrated as the Girls' Festival.

A display of beautiful dolls is the main feature of the celebrations. The ceremonial dolls are usually handed from generation to generation within a family, and are placed on display in the best room of the house. In addition to the dolls, exquisitely crafted miniature household articles are also displayed. The dolls most highly valued are the 'Daini-Sana' which represent the Emperor and Empress, both dressed in elaborate court attire. When the festival is over, the articles are carefully packed away and stored until the next year.

Holi (H)

Holi is the most colourful of Hindu festivals. It is a spring festival celebrated on the full moon day of the month of Phalguna (February-March). It falls when the season is neither hot nor cold and the trees bloom with different kinds of flowers.

According to legend, a mighty king named Hiranya Kashipu once ruled on the earth. His arrogance grew to such an extent that he declared himself to be a god and ordered his people to worship him. But Prahlad, the king's only son, refused to accept him as a god, as he had firm belief only in Rama. To punish his son, the King took different severe measures and even tried to kill him, but all the time Prahlad was saved as he uttered the name of Vishnu. At last, Prahlad's aunt, Holika, claiming that she was fireproof, took the child in her lap and sat in the fire to burn him alive. When the flames died down, the King found the child was safe but his aunt had perished in the fire.

Another legend associated with Holi is about the destruction of the handsome Kama, the god of love, by Shiva. In south India, the songs sung during Holi include the lamentations of Rati, Kama's wife.

According to another account, the festival of Holi was instituted to commemorate the destruction by Krishna of a female demon called Putana. When Krishna was a baby, his uncle Kansa, who was his enemy and the King of Mathura, ordered a general massacre of all children in order to destroy him. One of Kansa's agents was a female fiend named Putana, who assumed human form and went about the country sucking to death every child she found; but the infant Krishna, knowing her to be a fiend, sucked her blood and thus destroyed her. Those who attribute the origin of all festivals to seasonal cycles maintain that Putana represents winter and her death and cremation, the cessation of winter.

The festival takes two days for its observance. On the first day, a bonfire is lit either in the evening or during the night. The effigy of Holika is placed in the centre of the pile and a ministering brahmin recites verses in the worship of Holi before setting it on fire. People then return to their homes.

On the second day, from early morning till noon, people, irrespective of caste and creed, amuse themselves by throwing handfuls of coloured powder on their friends and relatives; or they spray coloured water with sprayers. The damage to people's clothes is taken in good spirit. The same evening, people exchange sweet-meats and friends embrace and wish each other good luck. The children and the young touch the feet of their elders to express their reverence.

Holla Mohalla (S)

In 1680 at Anandpur, India, Guru Gobind Singh, the tenth guru of the Sikhs, introduced the festival of Hola Mohalla as an alternative to the Hindu festival of Holi. There are displays of swordsmanship, horsemanship, archery, wrestling competitions, display of weapons and poetic symposia, making it a very colourful festival in the Sikh calendar.

Mothering Sunday (C)

This is held on the fourth Sunday in Lent. It was considered to be a break in the solemnities of Lent, being a cheerful day when girls in service visited their mothers, taking simnel cakes as presents. These cakes were generally kept until Easter. People in villages also went to the Mother Church to give gifts. Today it is celebrated by people buying cards and flowers for their mother and giving her a day of rest. Churches often provide flowers and cards for children to give to their mothers.

Shab-i-Miraj (M)

Historical Background

Shab-i-Miraj means the night of ascent. It is blessed night when the Holy Prophet of Islam was spiritually transported to heaven and reached such a high stage of nearness to God Almighty as was beyond human mind to conceive. The ascent took place in the fifth year of the call, about seven years before Hijra. The journey was with a vision of the highest type. On the way to meeting God, the Holy Prophet met Adam, Abraham, Moses, Jesus and some other prophets. The purpose of this spiritual ascent was to confirm the status of the Prophet of Islam, a position which all Muslims believe is impossible to attain by any other human being. It is related that even Gabriel, the Angel who was accompanying the Prophet, remarked at one stage, 'I am forced to stop here. I cannot go any further but you, O Messenger of Peace and friend of the Master of the World, continue your glorious ascent.'

It is also related that the Holy Prophet continued his journey until he was very close to the throne of God and attained the utmost nearness to him. After having drunk fully at the divine fountain of spiritual knowledge, he came down to impart that knowledge to mankind.

Celebrations

According to popular belief Miraj, or spiritual ascension, took place on the twenty-seventh day of Rajab. Muslims celebrate the occasion by holding prayers and reminding themselves of the high morals taught during this night's journey. In some Muslim countries, the houses, streets and especially the mosques are decorated with colourful pennants and bunting, and at night, they are well illuminated by means of electric lights, candles or even oil lamps. In the evening, worshippers assemble in the mosques, and there often is a speaker to address the pious crowd at this holy event. After the ceremony is over, sweets are distributed to all. Most of this holy night is spent in prayer, and many wealthy Muslims share some of their wealth by distributing money and food amongst the poor and destitute.

St Patrick's Day (C)

The patron saint of Ireland is remembered and honoured for his work as a missionary and evangelist. Legend says that as a teenager he was carried off to Ireland from England and later escaped and returned home as a priest to introduce the Christian faith. He built a monastry at Armagh. The Irish celebrate this day as a public holiday and wear shamrocks, which are also reminders of the Holy Trinity. The deep historic links of Catholicism and nationalism in Ireland are reflected in the St Patrick's Day processions, speech-making, drama and musical activities. In North America and in the countries where Irish missionaries have been active, celebrations are enthusiastically pursued.

Baha'i New Year (B)

March 21 is the first day of the Baha'i year, and is a time of rejoicing, as it also signals the end of the fast. It begins at sunset on March 20, and can take any form, provided there are a few prayers, and then there can be dancing, a musical performance or other celebrations.

Higan (Bd)

The spring and autumn equinoxes are important days in the Japanese calendar. They not only mark the seasonal changes but also symbolise the spiritual transition from the world of suffering (samsara) to the world of enlightenment (nirvana). Dead friends and relatives are particularly remembered at these times and special ceremonies are held to transfer merit to the departed.

Ramanavami (H)

The festival of Ramanavami is celebrated throughout India to commemorate the birth of Shri Rama, who was born to King Dasharatha of Ayodhya on the ninth lunar day in the bright fortnight of Chaitra (March–April). It is observed with sanctity and fasting. On this day, temples are decorated, religious discourses are held, and the 'Ramayana' (the life story of Rama) is recited in most Hindu homes. Thousands of devotees throng to temples which have 'darshana' (visualization of the deity) of the beautiful images of Rama enshrined there.

Palm Sunday (C)

This marks the beginning of Holy Week, the last week of Jesus's life, and celebrates the story of Jesus entering Jerusalem on a donkey (St Mathew 21, 1–9).

Processions are made around churches and between churches, carrying and distributing palms. Churches are usually decorated with palm or willow. Palm crosses are often given out.

Maundy Thursday (C)

This day commemorates the Last Supper which Jesus shared with his disciples where he gave the commandment to 'Love one another' and he washed their feet and instituted the Eucharist. (Maundy comes from the Latin word 'mandatum' meaning command.)

In Britain, Edward III annually washed and kissed the feet of the poor, but now the reigning sovereign gives money to the poor instead.

Christian people usually attend Holy Communion on this day and treat it as personal preparation for Good Friday.

April

April Fool's Day (Sec)

All Fool's Day – the 'fun' day when people are tricked by others or sent on silly errands, is observed in many countries in Europe and Asia.

The origin of these practices is obscure. One explanation as to why it is so widespread is that April 1 marked the end of the spring equinox, when celebrations were held to mark the period when the sun's rays fall vertically on the equator, and day and night are of equal length all over the earth.

According to some British historians, April 1 marks the end of the New Year celebrations in the old calendar when New Year's Day was the March 25. Yet another explanation offered is that it is a remnant of an old Celtic rite.

Good Friday (C)

The Friday before Easter Day on which the anniversary of the crucifixion of Christ is kept. It is a day of fast, abstinence and penance in some churches, but in others, notably the Free Churches, it has become a feast day.

Services are usually held in churches, sometime between noon and 3.00 pm when as Mark (15, 33–4) says, Jesus was on the cross. There are often united services and processions and passion plays portraying the Easter story.

Hot cross buns are eaten. They used to be kept specially for Good Friday, although they originated in pagan times with the bun representing the moon and its four quarters.

It is called Good Friday because Christians believe that because Jesus died they can gain forgiveness for their sins and everything will be right between them and God. His love and sacrifice are remembered.

Shab-e-Bharat (M)

This day falls about a fortnight before Ramadhan, and is traditionally celebrated in anticipation and preparation for the month of Ramadhan. Muslims fast and spend the night in prayer, as God is said to make a record of all the good and bad actions of man and to dispose their fate according to their actions.

31

Originally intended by the Prophet of Islam as an occasion for prayerful vigils and fasting, this has developed into a joyous festival celebrated in many parts of the world, when sweets, halva (sweet-meats made of sesame flour and honey) and bread are specially prepared and distributed to friends and to the poor.

Pesach or Passover (Jw)

This celebrates the deliverance of the children of Israel from Egypt where they were held as slaves.

The festival lasts for eight days, during which no bread, cakes or similar foodstuffs may be eaten, and on Matzoth unleavened bread is substituted for these.

The first two and last two days are particularly holy, and Jewish children do not attend school on these days.

On the eve of the first two days, special celebrations, called the Seder, are held in Jewish homes when families gather together for a festival meal preceded by recounting the story of the exodus from Egypt.

Holy Saturday (C)

This is the last day of Holy Week, once known as the 'Great Sabbath' and now also known as Easter Eve. It remembers Christ resting in the tomb.

Easter Sunday (C)

This is the most important festival in the Christian Church, celebrating the resurrection of Jesus.

The word Easter is connected with the Anglo Saxon spring goddess Eostre, and it seems that Christian celebrations displaced the pagan festival. The custom of giving eggs is an ancient one celebrating new life. People often spring clean or decorate and make a fresh start at Easter. New clothes are worn and there are Easter parades.

The date of Easter is determined by the paschal full moon and can be anywhere between 21 March and 25 April. There was early controversy whether Easter should follow the fixed lunar month and be celebrated at the time of the Jewish Passover, and various churches celebrated it at different times. The Alexandrian calculation was accepted in 325, but in the fourth and fifth centuries, the Roman Church disagreed. In Britain the Celtic churches had their own methods of calculations, but the Roman method was adopted by the Synod of Whitby in 664.

Easter is often celebrated with a midnight mass where the priest lights one candle and all the congregation follow and say 'Christ is risen'. Dawn services and outdoor services are quite common on Easter Day.

Qingming Festival (Ch)

Qingming (pronounced Chingming), or the Tomb-sweeping Festival, is not fixed by the lunar calendar, but occurs on the day the sun's longitude passes fifteen degrees at the start of one of the 24 sections of the solar year.

From early in the morning people visit their ancestors' shrines and tombs, carrying with them offerings of incense, joss paper and food cooked specially for the dead. Family members sweep the tombs of their loved ones, clear the ground of weeds, plant a new tree and repaint faded inscriptions on the tombstone. Joss paper is distributed around the tombs as a mark of their visit. Imitation paper money or gold, and paper clothes may be burnt as sacrificial gifts for the ancestors.

The festival is not usually celebrated in Britain, though many overseas Chinese return home sometimes for New Year and Qingming.

Hana Matsuri (Bd)

This festival commemorates the Buddha's birthday according to the Zen Buddhist tradition. In Japan, images of the infant Buddha are washed with a special sweet tea made from hydrangea leaves. In large temples great numbers of priests take part in these rituals.

Baisakhi/Vaisakhi (S)

Baisakhi is the north Indian harvest festival celebrated in the spring season. At that time wheat, the staple crop of the area, is ready for harvest and the farmer celebrates the fruit of his hard work with song and bangra dance (harvest-folk dance). It is also the New Year's Day in the state of Punjab and it usually falls on April 13 (occasionally on April 14 as in 1983).

The founder of the Sikh faith, Guru Nanak, started his missionary travels on this day, and so the third guru, Amar Das, asked his disciples to gather together on this day to celebrate it as a special festival, distinct from other faiths, to give the Sikhs a separate identity.

This carried on till the Baisakhi of 1699, when Guru Gobind Singh, the tenth guru, chose it to become the birthday of the Sikhs. Earlier he had sent commands to his followers, spread in the various parts of India, to gather together on Baisakhi Day, 1699. They came from far and wide and on the actual day itself, over a hundred thousand had assembled for the morning prayer at Anandpur (which literally means the town of bliss) which had been founded by Guru Gobind Singh's father, the ninth guru, Teg Bahadur. After the early morning prayers, the Guru addressed the congregation, then drew out his sword in a flash and demanded the head of a Sikh who would be willing to die for his faith. This was a strange demand coming from a guru who had won the hearts of his followers by helping the needy, the oppressed and the down-trodden.

Some panicked and left the congregation, others stayed, but such was the silence that one could hear a pin drop. Then one man, Daya Ram, offered his head to the Guru. He was taken outside the congregational hall by the Guru, the congregation heard the strike of the sword. The next moment, the Guru was back in the congregation with the same sword dripping with blood, and demanded another head. There was consternation in the audience, yet another man mustered courage and offered his head to the Guru. It happened five times in all. Then the Guru brought all those men back to the congregation hall, adorned in identical attire, and it is said that there was a certain aura around them. Another remarkable fact was that the men's names symbolised: kindness, righteousness, courage, steadfastness and leadership – values which all Sikhs are encouraged to believe in and uphold.

Guru Gobind Singh then baptised them with a special nectar, which he prepared in a steel bowl and to which his wife added sugar crystals. The mixture was then stirred by 'Khanda', the doubled-edged sword. Later on the Guru asked those Sikhs to baptise him. Thus was born what is known as the brotherhood of the Sikhs, the 'Khalsa' – a democratic arrangement in which the Guru and the Sikhs became equal participants.

After the initiation ceremony, the Guru asked them to follow a code of conduct which consisted of having the second name 'Singh' (which means lion) for men and 'Kaur' (princess) for women; practising equality and treating the human race as one; and wearing the five symbols. These symbols all have names starting with the letter 'K' in original Punjabi: 'Kes' – natural uncut hair, 'Kanga' – comb, 'Kara' – steel bangle, 'Kachahara' – traditionally-sewn shorts and 'Kirpan' a small dagger.

After Guru Gobind Singh, the Sikhs laid the foundation of the first fort to protect the holy temple at Amritsar on this day.

Baisakhi of 1919 is famous for what is known amongst the Sikhs as the Jallianwala Bagh massacre, when General Dyer, the Commissioner of Amritsar, considering it to be a political meeting, fired on a large crowd of men, women and children who had congregated in the walled park to celebrate this historic day. These days it is celebrated amongst the Punjabis all over the world as a religious, social and political occasion.

Sinhala and Tamil New Year's Day (T)

This is a time of great merry-making, and it is customary for people to be lavish in their hospitality on this day. Special sweet-meats and delicacies are prepared and people dress in their finery to participate in the various celebrations.

In Sri Lanka, New Year's Eve is also celebrated as a public holiday.

Songkrar Day (Th)

This is also celebrated as the Thai New Year. The main feature of the celebrations is the water festival. Many colourful spectacles such as boat races, parades, pageants and the appearance of the Songkrar Princess on a splendidly caparisoned wooden horse, are also associated with this festival.

On the last day of the festival, a drum and bell are simultaneously sounded three times in temples all over the land. As the vibrations die away the festivities come to an end for another year.

For the past 40 years or so, Thai New Year has been celebrated on December 31, though there remains an historic link with old April celebrations.

Vish u – The Malayalam New Year (H)

Vish u is celebrated by Hindus in Kerala (a state in south-west India) as the New Year. This festival coincides with spring and the beginning of the zodiacal cycle when the sun enters the sign of Aries.

Preparations for this festival start the day before, when the house is cleaned and an artistic arrangement of beautiful and auspicious objects is created in the room (or area) where the family deities are enshrined. The items used in this arrangement include flowers (especially yellow laburnums), fruit (especially the yellow citrus variety), vegetables such as pumpkins, coconuts, rice, polished brass and bronze lamps, a small mirror, a gold ornament and silver coins.

Children do not participate in the preparations and are generally not allowed to see the display until the next day, when they are awakened at dawn and led with their eyes closed to the 'Puja' room. Thus, the first sight to greet their eyes on New Year's Day is this beautiful arrangement. They are then presented with new clothes and gifts of money.

A feast, to which friends and relatives are invited, is an essential element in the day's festivities.

Yom Hashoah (Jw)

This day commemorates the victims of the Nazi Holocaust before and during the Second World War. Services of remembrance are held with special prayers of mourning and the lighting of memorial candles.

Ramadhan (M)

Fasting is one of the five pillars of Islam, and the month of Ramadhan is the ninth month of the Muslim calendar, when Prophet Mohammed chose the hottest time of the year to be spent restfully in prayer and meditation.

Muslims do not worship Mohammed, but they do regard him as the greatest Prophet of God, as he was the last one to come on earth and he was the one who actually completed the message which was left incomplete by former prophets. The encounter with the Angels is reserved only to the chosen ones and the messengers of God. They received their messages mainly through the Archangel Gabriel, who is described as powerful and honest, and is named in the Quran as the Holy Spirit, who carried God's messages to God's blessed prophets including Noah, Ibrahim, Lot, Ismail, Ishak, Yakoub, Yousuf, Musa (Moses), Haroun, El-Azer, Zakariya, Yahya (John) and Isa (Jesus).

Ramadhan is a very special month, as it is the month in which the Quran was first revealed as God's guidance to mankind. To mark their celebration and their gratitude, Muslims sacrifice some of their daytime material pleasures as an offering to the merciful God.

It is the sacrificial abstention from the material pleasures of food and water from dawn to sunset, while abstaining in the meantime from evil deeds. Fasting enables the rich to enter the experience of poverty and to teach the value of self discipline.

The Quran states:

'O ye who believe fasting is prescribed for you as it was prescribed for those before you, so that you may guard against evil.' (2, 184).

The fast is obligatory for every healthy, adult Muslim, male or female, but there are certain exemptions: for a sick person, a person who is travelling, a pregnant woman or one who is breastfeeding her child, or one who finds the severity of the fast hard to bear on account of age or other infirmity. When the reason for exemption is only temporary, as with an illness from which the person recovers, the number of days missed are later made up. Should the cause of exemption continue over a lengthy period of time or become permanent, as in the case of the infirm and elderly, the exemption is absolute, but the person concerned, if he can afford to, should arrange to provide food for a poor person for the whole month or give the equivalent amount in charity known as fidya.

Fasting during this month is to make man realise his many blessings and is a means of showing his thanksgiving and gratitude to God.

While the reward for every good action is prescribed by God and is written down by the recording angels, the reward for fasting is awarded and recorded by God himself. It is a month of communal worship when the Quran is read often, as it is believed that it was revealed around the twenty-seventh day of Ramadhan.

Yom Ha'atzmaut (Jw)

A modern festival celebrating Israel's independence.

The First Day of Ridvan (B)

The most important day in the Bahai year

After the death of the Bab (the Gate), his followers were known as the Babis, and they gradually came to look upon one of his followers, Baha'u'llah, as their leader. The Moslem authorities decided to kill off the movement altogether by sending the leader into exile to a series of countries belonging to the Ottoman Empire. The first stage of his exile was in Baghdad, in what is now Iraq, but they gave no indication at that time as to his next destination. Meanwhile he camped in the open, in large tents in a public park, accompanied by an ever-growing crowd of Babis who wanted to be with him until the last possible moment. They were grieving at the imminent parting, but at some time during their stay in the park, he informed them that he was the one promised to them by the Bab, as 'Him whom God shall make manifest', and the weeping changed to ecstasy and joy, as everyone realised that they had been privileged to meet the Promised One, even if only briefly before they would lose him. In their joy they called the park 'the garden of Paradise', which is equivalent to Ridvan, in the Persian language. This was the momentous birth of the Baha'i Faith, the Revelation given to Baha'u'llah (the Glory of God), during his incarceration in a filthy dungeon some years previously, but which he kept a secret until this time of the Ridvan festival. His advent is the culmination of all the promises of all religions, and there are many passages in all the Holy Books which relate to this time as being the time of the reconciliation of all faiths, and of universal peace as man comes to maturity. The time of prophecy is over, and the age of fulfilment begins. The founders of all previous faiths are revered as 'sitting on the same throne', and thus unity can become a reality.

On this day, throughout the world, the believers in every town, city or village, meet to celebrate and to hold their annual elections for the nine members of their community to serve on the local spiritual assembly for one year. No canvassing is allowed, and the ballotting is secret, resting solely upon the good character and spiritually of those elected.

St George's Day (C)

St George became patron saint of England during the reign of Edward III, when the Order of the Garter was founded under the saint's patronage. Although once a very prominent holy day in the Christian calendar, St George's Day is today celebrated mainly by special parades and rallies. Many legends have been built up around the figure of St George, but all that is known with a degree of certainty is that he suffered martyrdom in Palestine before the reign of the Roman Emperor Constantine where he may have been a soldier in the Roman Army.

Ninth Day of Ridvan (B)

On the ninth day of Ridvan, the family of Baha'u'llah finished their preparations for the journey, and joined him. Prayers are said, and Baha'i history books may be read, etc.

May
May 1 (C)

May Day is an old folk festival which later acquired religious significance, but like many other festivals its origins are disputed. According to one legend it stems from the Roman Festival to Maia, the mother of Mercury, in whose honour sacrifices were made on the first day of her month, accompanied by considerable merry-making.

May Day celebrations are also associated with the beneficent qualities ascribed to tree spirits. This explanation suggests that May Day festivities are relics of the ancient custom of tree worship.

In medieval England, May Day was a public holiday when most villages arranged processions, with all those participating carrying green boughs of sycamore and hawthorn. The most conspicuous element in the procession would be the May pole - a young tall tree, stripped of its branches and decorated with garlands of flowers and ribbons.

May Day celebrations did not find favour with the Church and devout Christians for a long time, and when Oliver Cromwell came to power all festivities were forbidden. It was only later when Charles II came to the throne that the customary merry-making associated with this folk festival was revived.

Towards the end of the nineteenth century, May 1 became known as Labour Day, and is commemorated in many parts of the world with military parades and political rallies.

Twelfth Day of Ridvan (B)

Twelfth day of Ridvan. Baha'u'llah and his family left to go over the mountains, and through the winter snows, to the shores of the Black Sea, going on by boat and landing at Constantinople; then via Adrianople to Gallipoli, and by sea to Alexandria, and finally, they were shipped to Akka, where he was confined to the old prison barracks, in a room looking out over the sea, with not a green tree in sight. The Israelis have nowadays given this room to the Baha'is, where it is visited by Baha'i pilgrims from around the world, but nobody else may go there.

Vaisakhapuja or Wesak (SL)

This is the most important festival in the Theravada Buddhist tradition. It commemorates three important events in the Buddha's life, namely his birth, enlightenment and death.

This is a time when people try especially hard to live up to the teachings of the Buddha. Kindness and generosity are two virtues that are particularly emphasised.

In all Theravada Buddhist countries, the festival is marked by much colour and gaiety. Homes are cleaned and decorated for the occasion. People visit temples to make offerings, and statues of the Buddha are washed with scented water. Streets and homes are lit with lanterns, and in Sri Lanka, there are various street entertainments and pageants. In Thailand, the day's celebrations usually come to an end with candle-lit processions around the local temples.

Lag B'Omer (Jw)

On the second day of Passover in ancient Israel, the first sheaf was cut of the barley harvest and offered up in the Temple. This started the counting of the Omer (a measure of the grain) leading to Shavout. The Jewish people were commanded to count the days during these seven weeks.

During this period there was plague among numerous pupils of the great Mishnaic scholar, Rabbi Akiva. The plague ceased on the thirty-third day of the Omer (Lag B'Omer) and therefore Jews traditionally observe this day as a minor festival.

School may be attended.

Boys' Festival (J)

Since World Ward Two, May 5 has been designated a national holiday in Japan and is known as Kodomo no Hi or Children's Day.

Paper or cloth streamers in the shape of a carp are hoisted on a wooden pole in the yard or garden. Several legends account for the choice of the carp, the most popular being based on the fact that this fish has great energy, power and determination to overcome obstacles and is therefore a fitting example for young boys.

This day is as much a day of festivity for small boys as March 3 is for girls in Japan.

Ascension Day (C)

This is kept on the Thursday which is the fortieth day after Easter. It commemorates Christ's last earthly appearance to his disciples after the resurrection and his ascension into heaven into divine glory, which traditionally happened on the Mount of Olives (See Mark 16, 19). (Luke 24–51 and Acts 1, 1–11).

The purpose of the commemoration is to remember that Christ's spirit lives on. In the Western Church the paschal candle lit during Easter is extinguished on Ascension Day in commemoration of Christ's departure from the apostles.

Lailat-ul-Qadr – Twenty-seventh Ramadhan (M) (The Night of Decrees)

This occasion falls on the eve of the twenty-sixth fast during the month of Ramadhan. It was on this night that the Holy Quran was revealed to the Prophet Mohammed by the Archangel Gabriel, thus it is so important that it is known as 'The Night of Power' which in Arabic is 'Lailat-ul-Qadr'.

The Holy Quran states:

'This month of Ramadhan is the month in which the Quran began to be revealed, the Book which comprises guidance and divine sign which discriminate between truth and falsehood.......' (2.186).

Prophet Mohammed was 40 years of age when he first received a revelation in a small cave in Mount Hira, which is a short distance away from Mecca. The Muslims believe that it is during this night that the earth was filled with angels, led by the Archangel Gabriel, to reveal the first verses of the Quran to Mohammed and signal the start of his mission:

'Read in the name of God, who created man from clinging cells, read for your God is the most generous, who taught man with the pen, taught man what he knew not.' (96:1–5)

It is significant that the first verses called for people to learn God's knowledge, and that it was Mohammed who was chosen to carry the Quran to mankind. The revelation continued until his death, for a period of about 23 years.

The whole month of Ramadhan is a period of spiritual training wherein believers devote much of their time to fasting, praying and reciting the Holy Quran and remembering God (Allah), as well as giving charity and good will. The last ten nights, especially, are spent in worship and meditation, and the more devout Muslims retreat to the mosque for this time and spend their time solely in the remembrance of Allah. They join the congregation at prayer times and for 'Taraweeh' (special prayers recited with Isha Salat in the evenings).

Devoting their time so fully to the remembrance of Allah, they hope to receive the divine favours and blessings connected with this blessed night. It is related that when the last ten days of Ramadhan began, Mohammed used to stay awake the whole night and was most diligent in worship. Thus Muslims spend this night in remembrance of Allah, asking forgiveness for their shortcomings. They have a firm belief that God accepts the prayers of the supplicant readily during this night.

Juma-tul-Wida (M)

This is the last Friday of the month in Ramadhan, the holy month of refined celebration, that is eagerly awaited by Muslims and missed when it ends. It is also a month of brotherhood and communal worship, as well as great spirituality, charity, peace and happiness. It is a day that marks the end of Ramadhan, and like a respectable visitor, Ramadhan is given a great welcome and likewise a special farewell.

Otherwise, Friday is the Muslim's holy day or Day of Assembly. At midday, they gather at the mosque to pray together and listen to the imam preach his sermon. Work is carried out as normal before and after Friday prayers. Before performing the actual prayer, or handling the Holy Quran, shoes are removed and one performs a Wozoo (holy wash) whereby one cleanses oneself before touching the Holy Quran or doing any pious act. Friday sermons are about Muslims' responsibilities and obligations, and strengthen the spiritual bond between the believers.

The Quran says:

'O ye who believe, when the call is made for Prayer on Friday, hasten to the remembrance of God and leave off all business, that is better for you, if you only knew.' (62:10).

Muslims gather at the mosque to pray together and listen to the imam preach his sermon (khutba) at noon every Friday. But this particular Friday is significant as it is the last Friday of the holy month, and a feeling of both sadness and happiness is experienced, as all the excitement of the month comes to an end, and the people look forward to its return after a year

Christian Aid Week (C)

This is a week in which Christians focus on the need to care both spiritually and materially for people everywhere. Third World countries are especially remembered both in special prayers and the raising of funds. The organisation of 'Christian Aid' usually has a theme for raising money, such as the provision of wells for villages.

Eid-ul-Fitr (M)

Eid is an Arabic word which means a day which returns often. There are two days in the year that are declared public holidays in Muslim countries. One is Eid-ul-Fitr (at the end of Ramadhan) and the other is Eid-ul-Adha which comes about ten weeks after the first Eid.

Eid-ul-Fitr is celebrated at the end of a period of fasting (the holy month of Ramadhan). There is a lot of excitement when the moon is sighted, a joyous surge runs through the hearts of all Muslims, young and old, in anticipation of one of the most joyful Eid festivals. Friends and relations exchange good wishes and blessings with each other. All the necessary preparations are made – shops are opened till late, streets and homes are decorated, and the general preparations for the next day get under way.

The next day, after rising early and having a bath, they wear new clothes (or their best clothes) and a special non-alcoholic perfume called 'athar'. They are treated to a special breakfast which includes a sweet dish of 'sheer-kurma' – vermicelli cooked in milk with dried dates, raisins, almonds and other nuts.

Eagerly, they proceed towards the 'Eidgah', which is the central mosque of the city, or to a specified open space that will accommodate the congregation. Separate enclosures are provided for women, because Islam does not permit the free intermingling of men and women. As was the practice of the Holy Prophet Mohammed, they go to the Eidgah generally by one route and return by another.

Eid prayer and Friday prayer is always offered in congregation, but no Adhan or Iqamat (introductory announcement of the prayer or exhortation) is called out for this service.

The prayer commences with the imam calling out 'Allah-o-Akbar' (Allah is the Greatest) aloud. When the prayer is over, a sermon is delivered by the imam, which generally includes the historical background and spiritual significance of the festival. After the service the worshippers greet each other by saying 'Eid Mubarak' and hug each other or just shake hands. The spirit of Eid is one of peace, forgiveness and of brotherhood, so after performing their duty, they return home happy and contented. The women prepare some exotic dishes as this is a big day of celebration. They have friends and relations to join them for meals. Gifts and greetings are exchanged, and although it is an occasion for joy and happiness, it is certainly not an occasion to indulge in frivolity, over-eating and mere pursuit of pleasure. The main purpose is always to seek the pleasure of God by glorifying him and rendering thanks to him for having enabled them to perform their duties.

It is a family day in the smaller as well as the wider sense, when Muslims visit friends and relatives to exchange greetings and good wishes. The joy and happiness of the occasion originate mainly from managing to complete the Ramadhan fasting and in being nearer to God.

Whit Sunday or Pentecost (C)

This is held on the fiftieth day after Easter and commemorates the gift of the Holy Spirit to the followers of Christ. It is often called Pentecost because when the disciples received the Holy Spirit and began to go out and preach about Jesus it was the Jewish festival of Pentecost.

Because it marked the first preaching about Jesus, it is called the birthday of the Christian Church. It is a favourite day for baptism. As converts are often dressed in white for baptism it was probably originally 'White Sunday'. It is marked by miracle or mystery plays and processions, particularly in the north of England where the 'Whit Walk' is common and new clothes are worn. It is a major Christian festival and celebrated as a Holy Day of Obligation in the Catholic Church.

Shavout (Jw)

This is the Jewish feast to celebrate the giving of the Ten Commandments on Mount Sinai. The festival is also connected with agriculture, and synagogues are usually adorned with flowers and plants. A portion of the Law, including the Ten Commandments, is read in synagogues, and children should not attend school on these two days.

Declaration of the Bab (B)

A spiritual seeker, Mullah Husayn, arrived at the town of Shiraz, and was met by a young siyyid (a direct descendant of the prophet Mohammed) wearing a green turban, who seemed to have been expecting him, and invited the traveller to his home. They spent the evening in prayer, and eventually the host revealed to his guest that all the signs given to him by his teacher, and the conditions laid down, were fulfilled in the young siyyid, as being the one whose advent all the wise people of Islam awaited. He called himself the Bab (Gate), and told Mullah Husayn that henceforth he would be known as the Bab-ul-Bab, which meant the Gate of the Gate. The Bab further declared 'This night, this very hour, shall, in the years to come, be regarded as one of the greatest festivals'. The very hour registered on the clock was two hours and eleven minutes after sunset in the year 1844. The Bab cautioned his visitor to tell nobody about this meeting, for seventeen other souls should spontaneously arise and find him, and together they would all constitute the 'Nineteen Letters of the Living', to bring the good news to all peoples. The Bab also said his sole purpose was to prepare the world for the Promised One of all faiths and the scriptural prophecies of the past, and he said, 'I am but a ring upon his finger'. The Baha'i Era dates from that year 1844 in the Western calendar. We celebrate the day with joy, and send cards.

Ascension of Baha'u'llah (B)

After imprisonment in Akka for two years in the old barracks, from which he wrote letters to the ruling monarchs and leaders of the world, Baha'u'llah, his son, Abdu'l-Baha (Servant of the Glory) and his family were moved to various locations, and Baha'u'llah was eventually given complete freedom, and enjoyed the great esteem of many people. He died peacefully. He lies buried in a mansion in Bahji, surrounded by a beautiful garden, laid out in such a way as to symbolise the order in the world of the future. Pilgrims to the Baha'i shrines in Israel, visit the tomb to pray there. They come from all quarters of the globe.

June
Corpus Christi (C)

Corpus Christi, literally the Body of Christ, is celebrated on the Thursday after Whit week. In the Catholic Church it is a Holiday of Obligation in which people are expected to attend church.

It celebrates the institution of the Eucharist at the Last Supper. The Eucharist is celebrated on the Thursday of Holy Week, but being placed then between the austerity of Ash Wednesday and the dramatic tragedy of Good Friday a joyous commemoration is difficult.

Guru Arjan Dev's Martyrdom Day (S)

Guru Arjan Dev, the fifth guru of the Sikhs, was the first Sikh martyr. By the time of his leadership, the Sikh faith had developed into a well organised and established religion, with missionary centres in all the major towns and districts of the north-west of India and Pakistan, particularly in the state of Punjab. Towns like Kartarpur, Goindwal and Amritsar had been established by the previous gurus where trading activities and skills flourished. New ceremonies and festivals had been set up in which women and lower castes were treated equally with higher castes. A strong Sikh community was taking shape.

Guru Arjan Dev strengthened the community by building Harimandir, the Golden Temple, the holiest shrine of the Sikhs in Amritsar, and he also compiled the Adi Granth, the Sikh Holy Book which was placed in the Sikh shrine for recitation and for singing.

The missionary activities of the Guru further strengthened the hold of the new faith amongst the people of the Manjha region (between the rivers Sutluj and Ravi in Punjab).

The spread of Sikhism was looked upon with suspicion by the ruling authorities who found a ready ally in Prithi Chand, the eldest brother of Guru Arjan who considered himself the rightful heir to his father's guruship, but was deprived of it by his father in favour of Guru Arjan.

It is said that a plot was hatched, as a result of which Guru Arjan was suspected of supporting the dissident Prince Khusrau against the Mughal Emperor Jahangir.

Guru Arjan was arrested, brought to Lahore, the capital of Punjab state at that time, and was executed in such a way that no blood was shed. After his death he is said to have been thrown into the river Ravi and his body was never recovered.

Guru Arjan is celebrated in Sikh history as an apostle of peace and learning, and the day of his martyrdom is celebrated as the victory of good over evil.

Dragon Boat Festival (Ch)

Duan Yang, or the Dragon Boat Festival, is celebrated on the fifth day of the fifth lunar month. It commemorates the suicide by drowning in 279 BC of Qu Yuan, a famous poet and high-ranking official. Legend has it that the peasants took out their dragon boats and rushed to save him, but in vain. In order to prevent the fish eating his body, they threw rice dumplings wrapped in bamboo leaves into the river. These dumplings are still made and eaten during the festival.

It also became the custom to hold races between dragon boats. These are very long narrow rowing boats, brightly painted like dragons with plenty of red and gold and with dragon's head at the prow. They are usually manned by rival crews from neighbouring villages. The races take place accompanied by men waving flags and the noise of beating gongs. Later, in the evening, the boats parade along the water bedecked with colourful lanterns.

The races are not held in Britain, but there is a spectacular international race held in Hong Kong.

Feast of St Peter and St Paul (C)

Saints Peter and Paul are seen as two powerful pillars of the Christian Church. Peter became the first Bishop of Rome, and Paul took the Christian message with vigour and eloquence to a new gentile audience.

This is a Holy Day of Obligation in the Catholic Church.

Poson (Bd)

This festival marks the bringing of Buddhism to Sri Lanka by the missionary Mahinda. The main feature of the celebrations is the Minindu Perahera, when important events in the life of Mahinda are re-enacted.

July
The Martyrdom of Bab (B)

During all the years of his brief Ministry from the age of 25 to 31, the Bab was hounded and persecuted by the divines of the prevailing state religion, and consigned to bleak prisons in obscure parts of Iran, in the hope that he and his teachings would be forgotten. Eventually he was condemned to death, and the story of his execution is most extraordinary and worth telling. One of his disciples begged to be allowed to share his fate, and this wish was granted. On the eve of the execution, the leader of the execution squad, a Christian, came to see the prisoner, and confessed to him that he did not personally harbour any grudge against him and did not want to kill him. The Bab said, 'If your intention be sincere, the Almighty is surely able to relieve you of your perplexity'. When the hour came, the Bab and his disciple were supended, face to face, by ropes passing under their armpits, from a prominent pillar in the barrack square of Tabriz. Thousands of people stood on the walls, jeering. An Armenian firing squad lined up and fired, and when the smoke cleared, the Bab had gone, but his disciple was standing against the wall, unhurt. Only the ropes had been severed, and the Bab was found back in his cell, dictating notes to a secretary. The soldiers were so shaken by the 'miracle, that they all refused to try again. In due course, a new regiment was called in and the prisoners again tied up. The Bab addressed the crowds in these words, 'Had you believed in me, every one of you would have followed the example of this youth, who stood in rank above most of you, and would have willingly sacrificed himself in my path. The day will come when you will have recognised me; that day I shall have ceased to be with you'. And so they fired again and this time the bodies were riddled with bullets, but the faces little marred. The bodies were eventually rescued from a moat outside the town into which they had been thrown, and were hidden by faithful believers until, years later, the remains were interred on Mount Carmel in Israel, beneath the lovely golden-domed building known as the Queen of Carmel. The execution was at noon and at that time all over the world, the Baha'is read special prayers for the occasion, turning to stand in the direction of Haifa. This is a 'no-work' day.

Obon (J)

A four-day festival celebrated in Japan to pay respect to the spirits of dead ancestors. Legend has it that the Buddha rescued the mother of one of his disciples on this day after she had been sent to one of the hells. Graves are cleaned and decorated with flowers. Incense is lit and prayers offered. The spirits of the dead are invited to return home and hemp reeds are burned to light the way. Special food is prepared for the honoured guests.

At the end of Obon, the Bon-Odori dances take place. This is a simple folk dance performed to the accompaniment of songs and drum beats.

Haj – Pilgrimage (M)

Haj is one of the five pillars of Islam. Haj is performed during the period from the eighth to thirteenth of Zul-Hijja. During this time pilgrims from all over the globe flock to Mecca in Saudi Arabia, and the finest example of true brotherhood of man is shown to the world, otherwise torn by political, economic, religious and cultural strife. A Muslim makes every effort to perform this pilgrimage at least once in a lifetime, whenever he finds the means to do so.

These are the important rituals associated with this ceremony.
1. Putting on Ihram. A male pilgrim has to discard his usual clothes and dress himself in two white sheets of seamless cloth. One sheet is wrapped round the waist covering the lower abdomen, while the other is slung over the left shoulder. The head remains bare. Women may dress themselves in simple clothes and are not required to cover their faces.
2. Performing seven circuits of the Kaabah, the pilgrims enter the great mosque. The Muslims' spirituality reaches a peak as they leave their worldly cares behind, clothe themselves in simple, humble, white sheets of cloth, and stand, rich and poor, master and servant, shoulder to shoulder, in concentric rings of prayer around the Kaabah, all raising their prayers to the One God who is unseen, but whose presence is felt everywhere. They walk round in an anti-clockwise direction, and all say the same phrase that the prophet Abraham said four thousand years ago, which is translated as follows:

'Here I am, my Lord, here I am,
Here I am. There is no associated with thee.
Thine is the kingdom,
There is no associate with thee.'

The Kaabah is a very simple, stone structure, cubic shaped, laying no claim to grandeur of size or beauty of architecture. It impresses by its very simplicity.
3. Performing the Sa'ee, which is going seven times between the two nearby mountains of Safa and Marwah, in commemoration of Hagar, the Egyptian wife of Ibrahim and mother of Ismael, in her attempts to look for water for her thirsty infant Ismael. The pilgrim then goes to drink water from the blessed well of Zam-Zam, that sprang out from underneath the feet of Ismael, in answer to his mother's prayer, and is still flowing to this day.
4. Visiting Mina, Arafat and Muzdalifah. On the eighth of Zul-Hijja, the pilgrims leave Mecca for Mina and spends the night there in prayer and meditation. On the ninth day, they go to Mount Arafat, the 'Mountain of Mercy', where God forgave Adam and Eve and led them back to each other. Being there with a repentant heart on the appointed date is all

that is required to earn total forgiveness, yet another example of God's mercy and compassion. They arrive there after midday, offer Zuhr and Asr prayers and remain at Arafat until sunset.

To stay at Arafat from post-meridian till sunset is regarded as an important ritual of Haj, as it is on this plain that man seeks pardon for his sins and returns from Haj as sinless as the day he was born. Pilgrims then proceed to Muzdalifah where Maghrib and Isha prayers are combined and the night is spent in praising God and in meditation. Some small stones are taken from here on the journey back to Mina after the morning prayer the next day. At Mina, the pilgrim stones the three places where Satan appeared to the prophet Abraham, trying to dissuade him from obeying God, as he was on his way to sacrifice his only son, Ismael. The stoning of the three places is to symbolise the Muslims' obedience to God, and their rejection of the Devil.

5.   On the tenth day of Zul-Hijja, the pilgrim sacrifices an animal that he can afford, such as a goat, sheep, cow or camel. This is known as the Feast of Sacrifice, thus commemorating the prophet Abraham's success in his test, demonstrating that he loved God more than he loved his son, when God stopped him sacrificing his son and offered him a fat ram to slaughter instead. The purpose of the sacrifice is to feed the poor, as well as one's friends, neighbours and oneself.

6.   After staying at Mina for the three days of the feast, the pilgrims return to Mecca for Tawaaf al Widaa, the farewell visit before departure.

7.   Pilgrims have their heads shaven or cut their hair short.

Pilgrimage is a time when Islam's history comes alive, especially when one remembers the prophet Mohammed's glorious struggle, resolve, tolerance and wisdom in fulfilling his message. Thus the pilgrims pay their respects by visiting him in the mosque at Medina where he is buried. They return with holy water, dates, and blessings for everybody.

Tish B'av (Jw)

A day of mourning for the destruction of the first and second Temples in Jerusalem.

Eid-ul-Adha (Bakra Eid) (M)
The Festival of Sacrifice

The Eid is celebrated with great solemnity and reverence everywhere. Like Eid-ul-Fitr, Muslims make preparations several days before the festival. The animals to be sacrificed are bought well before the Eid day by those who can afford to do so and are well looked after. These animals should be free from all physical defects and should be fully grown. In the case of a sheep or goat, one animal suffices for one household, whereas a cow or camel can be shared by seven.

The details of these events are mentioned in the Bible and in the Quran. It is narrated that Abraham saw a vision that he was slaying his only son Ismael. He mentioned the dream to his son Ismael and asked, 'What do you think of it?' Ismael replied, 'Father, do that which you have been commanded. You will find me God-willing and steadfast.' Being thus convinced that God demanded this sacrifice of his son, who was bestowed to him in his old age, he began to make the necessary preparations. Then Abraham received the revelation that he had indeed fulfilled his covenant, and on God's command, the angels brought a ram instead and put it in place of Ismael. Thus the animal was sacrificed, and this festival of sacrifices therefore urges all Muslims to follow the examples of Abraham, Hagar and Ismael and show perfect submission to God's commands.

Therefore Muslims – especially adults who have performed their pilgrimage – make this sacrifice.

A third of the meat is kept for the use of the household, and the remainder is distributed uncooked among the poor and sent as gifts to friends and relatives.

Many families get together and cook exotic dishes, both savoury and sweet, and rejoice with relations and friends. They wear new clothes and attend prayers at the big mosque called 'Eid Gah'.

Kandy Perahera (SL)

This is a ten-day festival celebrated in the ancient highland capital of Kandy in Sri Lanka. From the Temple of the Tooth, a casket containing a sacred tooth relic of the Buddha is paraded in a colourful procession of elephants, dancers and musicians.

Asalhapuha or Dhammacakka (Bd)

This festival falls on the full moon day of the month of Asalha. It celebrates the first sermon of Buddha and the setting of the Wheel of Truth (Dhammacakka) into the world.

August
Hijrat – Muslim New Year 1409 (M)

This is celebrated on the first of Muharram. Hijrat means leaving one place of residents for another. In the history of Islam, it happened when the Holy Prophet of Islam migrated from Mecca, where he and his followers were persecuted, to Medina where they were welcomed by the populace in AD 622. This event is known as Hijrat. The people of Medina welcomed him and his companions. The first mosque was built there, where he fulfilled his message of establishing the Islamic social order and code of practice.

The Muslim calendar is based on the lunar cycle, and in terms of the solar calendar, it is approximately eleven days shorter than the Gregorian calender year. It has twelve months to a year, and the first day of each month is determined by the sighting of the new moon on the previous night. The Lunar month consists of either 29 or 30 days; that is why the sighting of the moon becomes more important in deciding the dates of the festivals.

To calculate conversions from one calendar to another, the following formula is used:

$$G = H + 622 - \frac{H}{33}$$

$$H = G - 622 + \frac{G - 622}{32}$$

G = Gregorian Calendar.

H = Hegira, or migration of the prophet Mohammed from Mecca to Medina.

In fact, Islam has made use of both the lunar and solar systems of measuring time. Where worship is performed at different parts of the day, the solar system of reckoning time is used, as in the five daily prayers or for the beginning and breaking of the fast. Also, where worship is to be completed within a particular month or part of a month, the lunar system is used, as in the determination of the month of fasting or fixing the time of Haj or other festivals.

The names of the months of the Muslim calendar are listed on page 18. The first month, Muharram, the seventh, Rajab, and the last two, Zul-Qeda and Zul-Hijja, are considered sacred months and fighting during them is considered a sin.

The Holy Quran states:

'The number of months with Allah has been twelve by Allah's ordinance since the day he created the heavens and the earth. Of these, four are known as sacred.' (9.36)

The Quran also states:

'They ask thee, O Prophet, concerning the phases of the moon. Tell them: these alterations are a means of determining time for regulation of people's affairs and for the pilgrimage.' (2.190).

Muharram (M)

'Muharram' is the name of the first month of the Muslim year. The first day of Muharram is declared a public holiday in Muslim countries. The Muslim calendar dates from the year the Prophet Muhammed – under pressure of persecution from the Mecca unbelievers – accepted the believers invitation and emigrated to Medina in AD 622, where he fulfilled his message of establishing the Islamic social order and code of practice. The first ten days commemmorate the loss of many prominent members of the Prophet's family and a number of his followers, when they were surrounded by the force of Yazid, the Muslim ruler of that time, while they were on a journey. They were deprived of food and water and many of them were put to death. The incident happened at a place called Karbala in Iraq, in the 61st year of the Mijra (61 AH). In fact, after the death of the fourth caliph (Hasrat Ali), Muslims were divided in their opinion as to who should be their new caliph. As a result they fought with each other and there was a lot of bloodshed.

The tenth of Muharram (September 14) is a festival called Ashuraa and is especially remembered by the Shia sect as they observe this festival after Imam Hussain.

Ashuraa – Tenth Day of Muharram (M)

Some Muslim sects observe this festival with great respect, having prayers, talks and vigils, and singing dirges in memory of Imam Hussain, the grandson of Prophet Mohammed. It commemorates great tragedy at Karbala at Mecca in which Imam Hussain was brutally speared to death in the sixty-first year of the Hijra (AH), and when practically all of the Prophet's family including his son-in-law, Hazrat Ali, were annihilated.

Members of the Shia sect dress in black clothes as they spend the first ten days of the year in mourning. Assemblies are held every day for the first nine days, where Shia orators relate the incident of the death of Imam Hussain and his party in great detail, and on the tenth day of Muharram, large processions are formed and the devoted followers parade the streets holding banners and carrying models of the mausoleum of Immam Hussain and his people who fell at Karbala. They show their grief and sorrow by inflicting wounds on their own bodies with sharp metal pieces tied to a chain with which they scourge themselves, to depict the sufferings of the martyrs. It is a sad occasion and everyone in the procession chants 'Ya Hussain' with loud wails of lamentation. Usually, a white horse, beautifully decorated for the occasion, is also included in the procession, perhaps to mark the empty mount of Imam Hussain after his martyrdom.

During these ten days, drinking posts are also set up temporarily by the Shia community where water and juices are served to all, free of charge. It has also become customary to serve milk, or 'sharbat' (softdrinks) at these functions to remind Muslims of the way Imam Hussain and his followers were starved and tortured to death.

On this day, God saved Moses and his followers from the pursuing army of the self-appointed god, Pharoah. The Prophet asked his followers to honour this occasion by fasting. Muslims therefore fast on this day and remember the tragedies of the Prophet Mohammed's family and relations.

Onam (H)

Onam is celebrated as a harvest festival by people of all faiths in Kerala – the state at the south-western tip of India.

According to legend, Kerala was once ruled by the benevolent King Mahabali. The gods, jealous of his popularity, determined to teach him a lesson. Thus Vishnu – one of the Holy Trinity in the Hindu pantheon-appeared in the guise of a dwarf brahmin and begged the King for as much land as he could cover in three paces. The King immediately agreed, and in fact begged the Brahmin to take more land. Vishnu, however, could not be tempted and proceeded to measure out the three paces. The first step he took covered the heavens and the second the entire earth. For the third step, he placed his foot on the bowed head of the King, who had by this time realised the true identity of the dwarf Brahmin, and pushed him into the earth, first granting him the wish of being allowed to return once a year to visit his subjects.

On this day, therefore, people dress up in new clothes and decorate their homes with beautiful flower arrangements. A grand feast is prepared and food is distributed to the brahmins and to the poor and needy.

The festivities in the state are also marked by boat races. The normally quiet backwaters of Kerala are transformed as people line the banks along the route to cheer their favourite team.

The celebrations are brought to an end with fireworks displays.

Raksha Bandhan (H)

The Raksha Bandhan festival is celebrated especially in northern India in the month Sravana (July–August). The word Raksha signifies protection. The festival is also called Saluno.

Girls and married women tie a rakhi, made of twisted golden or simple yellow threads, on the right wrist of their brothers, for their welfare and also for protection from any evil influence, and in return they receive cash and gifts. This is an age-old festival, which strengthens the bond of love between brothers and sisters.

On this day, members of a Hindu family bathe very early and go to market to purchase rakhi and sweets from the colourful stalls, which spring up everywhere. The men, dressed in their best, and women in their bright costumes, first offer prayer to their daily deity. A man considers it a privilege to be chosen as a brother by a girl who ties a rakhi on his wrist. If the brother is not at hand, the rakhi is sent to him by post or passed on to him by someone. In some parts of India, women also tie rakhies to close friends and neighbours.

The brahmins, or the priestly class, also tie rakhi to their 'yajamanas', (patrons and clients), recite hymns for their safety and receive something in cash or kind from them.

The rakhi festival has a special appeal in India which extends to other non-Hindu communities. One story tells of how, during the Muslim rule, a beautiful Hindu queen called Padmini sought protection from the Mughal Emperor by sending him a rakhi. When Padmini was threatened by another Muslim king who had determined to marry her when he saw her reflection in the mirror, the Queen was defended against his invasion by the Mughal Emperor in response to the rakhi. To this day, rakhi from a woman is honoured even when the man is not a Hindu.

September
Janmashtami (H)

The popular festival of Janmashtami is observed throughout India at midnight, on the night of the new moon during the month of Bhadrapada (August–September). It is joyously celebrated in honour of Lord Krishna, who was born on this day, at Mathura in Uttar Pradesh.

On the festival day, all temples and many Hindu homes are beautifully and tastefully decorated to welcome the birth of divine chief, Krishna. His image is placed on a swing, in a decorated 'mandapa' (small pavilion). Every member of the family, including children, observes a fast for the whole day and only breaks it when the moon is visible at midnight, at which tie the small image of a crawling Krishna is first bathed in 'charnamrita' (curd mixed with milk, dry fruits and leaves of the 'tulsi' plant) and then the 'arati' is performed. (Arati is the veneration and supplication accompanied by circular movements of the lamp and by the throwing of flower petals) The 'prasada' is distributed to all present and thus the day-long fast is broken. (Prasada is symbolic communion in food, usually made of semolina, sugar and water).

The First Presentation of Adi Granth (S)

Adi Granth was presented to the Sikh congregation for the first time by the fifth guru, Guru Arjan Dev, in 1587. Before that, Gurbani (word of God revealed through Sikh gurus) of the first four gurus was written in four different parts. Guru Arjan Dev not only collected Gurbani of gurus but also the writings of Muslim fakirs (saints) and Hindu bhagats and saints (some of low castes) who believed in one God and the equality of all humans. He himself wrote a major part of Gurbani, which accounts for 2312 shabads (hymns), and compiled it in different ragas (musical modes). The first presentation of Adi Granth was made in Harmandir Sahib (Golden Temple) which was built by the fifth Guru in the town of Amritsar. He appointed Baba Budha Jee as the first granthi (priest). Gurbani from Adi Granth is read and sung by all Sikh congregations. Some Sikhs keep the Holy Book in their homes and read it morning and evening or whenever they can.

Rosh Hashanah (Jw)

On these two days, the New Year, the Jewish people are symbolically judged by God in Heaven, and the Ram's Horn, the Shofar, is blown to awaken the people to repentance.

These days are among those observed by all Jewish people and children should not attend school. Most Jews, wherever they happen to be, will attend synagogues.

Harvest Festival (C)

This is one of the oldest festivals known to man. After prayers for a good harvest, it seemed natural to give offerings or sacrifice part of the crops. The Jews celebrate three harvest festivals dating from their wanderings in the wilderness with Moses. In Christian Britain, harvest is an unofficial religious festival of thanksgiving usually observed on a Sunday in September or October to give thanks for the harvest being gathered in.

Since the middle of the last century, the custom of displaying fruits, vegetables and flowers in the Church of England and the Free Churches has developed, and these are later given to charitable causes.

In mediaeval times, Lammas Day, August 1, was a celebration of the offering of the first fruits (Duet 26, 1–11). A loaf made from the first grain was baked and used in the Eucharist. The service was called Loaf Mass, in Saxon 'Half Masse', which gradually became Lammas. The arrival of Lammas Day also meant that the Lammas Land in some village could be used for general grazing of stock by all villagers as the hay would have already been reaped. Country fairs were also held around Lammas Day.

When all the harvest had been gathered in, Harvest Home would be celebrated at the farmer's house, with a supper. The last of the corn would be twisted into a person or cross corn dolly. It was believed that the corn spirit was contained in the dolly and had to be kept alive during the winter and sown with the new corn to ensure a good harvest. It was often taken to the church for the harvest service before being hung in the barn. Some churches still have harvest suppers.

In seaside towns, churches may celebrate a harvest of the sea, and in some manufacturing towns, tools or machinery may now replace the traditional displays. Special hymns are sung and the Church of England has a special service.

Ganesh Chaturthi (H)

Ganesha, the elephant-headed god in the Hindu pantheon, is worshipped all over India as the remover of obstacles. His blessings are especially invoked before the start of any important enterprise. On this day, prayers are offered to the god along with specially prepared foods.

In the city of Bombay and in other parts of the state of Maharashtra, this festival has always been closely associated with a strong feeling of nationalism and is celebrated in a particularly dramatic manner. Gaily coloured and garlanded statues of the god are taken out in procession through city streets and are finally immersed in the sea to the accompaniment of loud chantings and music. 'Prasada' is then distributed to the gathering of devotees.

In parts of southern India, devotees of Ganesha believe that it is unlucky and inauspicious to look at the moon on this day. The belief has its origins in a myth referring to the god and his love of good food, especially 'laddus' (sweetmeats) and coconut. Thus, it is said, that when Ganesha was returning from a celestial banquet, he saw a reflection of the new moon in a pool of water. Mistaking it for a sliver of coconut, he stooped down from his mouse-drawn carriage to pick it up. Seeing this, the moon laughed loudly and Ganesha, highly offended, cursed her and all those who saw her on this day.

Yom Kippur (Jw)

This is the Day of Atonement, the tenth day from Rosh Hashanah. It is observed as a fast day from the eve of the day to nightfall on the day itself. During these 25 hours or so, no food or drink touches the lips of Jews and most Jewish people remain in the synagogue throughout the day in worship and contemplation.

Mid-Autumn Festival (Ch)

Zhong Qiu, the Mid-Autumn or Moon Festival, is held on the day of the full moon in the eighth month, which in a lunar month always falls on the fifteenth or sixteenth. It is one of the major festivals, and traditionally incense is burned and offerings of fruit such as melons, pomegranates, grapes and peaches together with mooncakes are made to the moon goddess and to the hare which lives in the moon.

The mooncakes commemorate an uprising against the Mongols in the fourteenth century when the call to revolt was written on pieces of paper embedded in the cakes. They are made of a pastry filled with bean paste or lotus seeds, and often contain solid duck egg yolks to represent the moon.

The festivities may include lion dances, and in the evening children form parades carrying multi-coloured lanterns. These may be made in many shapes from cars and planes to traditional animals such as the symbolic carp or mandarin ducks.

Mooncakes and lanterns are sold around this time in London's Chinatown, and there is usually a lion dance.

Higan (Bd)

See page 30 for information on this equinox festival.

Succott or Tabernacles (Jw)

Succott or Feast of Tabernacles. This is a nine-day (eight days in Israel) festival comme-morating the divine protection given to the Israelites during their wanderings through the wilderness. Temporary dwelling places (succott) are erected in the synagogue and meals are taken there. Palm and myrtle branches are waved, symbolic of God's universal presence. Seven circuits of the synagogue are made. The first, second, eighth and ninth are especially holy days, and the eighth involves prayers for rain and recalls the former temple ceremonies of drawing water.

This is a nine day-festival of which the first two and the last two days are periods when Jewish children should not attend school.

October
Simchath Torah (Jw)

This is the ninth and last day of Succott on which the cycle of the Reading of the Law in synagogues is completed for the year by reading the last section of the Book of Deutero-nomy, and another scroll is unwound from which is read the beginning of the Book of Genesis immediately, to demonstrate that the study of the Torah is an everlasting and continuous process.

There is much festivity to celebrate this event, and children play a prominent part in it.

The privilege of reading the last portion of the Law and beginning again is given to members of the synagogue who have been active on behalf of the community.

Chong Yang Festival (Ch)

Chong Yang, the ninth day of the ninth moon, also called Double Nine, commemorates an incident which is believed to have taken place on this day.

According to the legend, there were two friends who travelled together for many years pursuing their studies. One day, one of them had a premonition that on the ninth day of the ninth moon, the household of his friend would meet with a grave disaster. It could be avoided if the family left their home for the day and took refuge in the hills.

The friend did as he was advised and did not return home with his family until nightfall. On their return, they discovered that during their absence all the domestic animals had perished mysteriously. The same fate would have overtaken the family had they not fled to the hills. Since then, it has become customary for Chinese people to climb hills, towers and pagodas on Double Nine, which is also called the Day of Ascending Heights.

Chrysanthemums bloom in their splendour during this month and chrysanthemum wine and dishes are served as delicacies on this day.

Dussehra (H)

Dussehra, one of the most popular festivals in India, is celebrated all over the country for ten days in the month of Asvina (September–October). The festival, besides other minor functions, comprises the worship of the goddess Durga, during Navratri (Nine Nights), the 'Ram-Lila', 'Vijayadasmi' and Maha Ashtami.

Among the Hindu festivals, Durga Puja is unique. The festival starts on the first night of the Hindu month of Asvina. Durga is worshipped as Divine Mother or as Kumari, the virgin goddess. The Saktas, who consider the goddess as the supreme deity, worship a manifestation of the goddess on each of the Navratri nights. Usually, the images of the goddess are installed in uses or, in the case of community worship, in public places and worshipped by the performance of puja (worship), by katha and religious music. Katha is story-telling, and it is a favourite exercise in devotion among Hindus. A pandit, well versed in ancient lore, regales the congregation by reading passages from a text extolling the deity. He explains it to the audience with comments enlivened by many anecdotes and tales.

In the Punjab, the first seven nights of Navratri are considered a period of fast. According to a legend, malicious demons who ruled the Punjab forbade the people from eating anything, all the available food being consumed by the voracious brood. On this day, the people prayed to the goddess Durga who appeared in her war-like form and fought the demons for seven days and put them to flight. On the eighth, the goddess went among the people and asked them to feast themselves. In memory of this, the people of Punjab observe the first seven days of Navratri as a period of austerity, but on the eighth, ample amends are made by feasting.

In Gujerat, the celebration of Navratri, or Nine Nights, is marked by 'Garba', a dance performed by women. They joyfully dance around an earthern lamp placed on a stand, singing and clapping hands in rhythmic movements. In Tamil Nadu, the first three days of the festival are dedicated to the goddess Lakshmi, the next three days to the goddess Sarasvati. Durga worship is especially popular in Bengal. Both Hindus and non-Hindus worship her in the form of Kali. After nine nights (Navratri) of fast and worship, the images of Durga are taken out in procession and immersed in a tank, river or in the sea.

The main feature of Dussehra is the Ram-Lila based on the epic story of Ramayana. During this week, dramatic troupes perform plays based on the Ramayana.

On Vijaya-dasmi Day, which is the last day of the Dussehra festival, the worship of gods, especially Lord Rama, is done with fervour, and prayers are offered in every home. Poor people and the brahmins carrying navatras (small fresh offshoots of barley plants, which are sown in every house on the first day of festival), go to wealthy people to offer them stalks of navatras and receive alms in return.

Though celebrated all over India by common folk, Dussehra is chiefly a royal festival beloved of the ruling classes. With independence and the disappearance of the princes from the Indian political scene, these ancient pageants are dying out and the festival is becoming more democratic than regal. However, it is still considered of great importance by the displaced rulers.

The Birthday of the Bab (B)

He was born in 1819 in Shiras, Persia. As his father died when he was still a baby, he was brought up by a maternal uncle. One day he was sent home from school because his teacher considered that there was nothing more he could teach him. The uncle thought the child must have behaved badly, but the teacher said that the pupil knew more than he did – the fact being that he had innate knowledge. The Bab was a direct descendant of the Prophet Mohammed, and therefore was entitled to wear the traditional green turban. He has been described as being sweet and gentle mannered, of noble character, and great personal beauty. He was trained in commerce, and was known for his fair dealings.

The believers celebrate this event with reverence and joy, in community gatherings.

Eid Milad-un-Nabi (M)

This is the festival to commemorate the anniversary of the birth of the Holy Prophet Mohammed. It is celebrated on the twelfth day of Rabee-ul-Awwal. From the point of view of Muslims, this date marks the most important event in the history of the world. Mohammed is regarded as the last and the chief of the prophets, the perfect man to whom the Holy Quran was revealed, the best example, and the greatest benefactor of mankind. He is the person for whom God has proclaimed:

'Allah sends down his blessings on the Prophet, and his angels constantly invoke his blessings on him, do you O believers, also invoke Allah's blessings on him and offer him the salutation of peace.' (33:57)

The extent of festivities, on this occasion, is restricted because of the fact that the same day marks the anniversary of his death.

On this occasion, therefore, public meetings are held in the mosques, where religious leaders make speeches on different aspects of the life of this great man. The stories of the Prophet's birth, childhood, youth and manhood, character, teachings, sufferings and forgiveness of even his most bitter enemies, his fortitude in the face of general opposition, leadership in battles, bravery, wisdom, preachings and his final triumph through God's mercy over the hearts of the people, are narrated in detail.

Salutations and songs in his praise are recited. In some countries, streets, mosques and public buildings are decorated with colourful buntings and pennants and well illuminated at night.

Devout Muslims give large sums to charity. Feasts are arranged and rice and meat dishes are served to the guests and also distributed among the poor. In some big cities, large processions are alse formed, and people in jubilant mood chant verses in praise of the Holy Prophet Mohammed.

Some Muslims, however, do not celebrate this occasion as his birthday or death anniversaries as they believe such celebrations are not part of Muslim society as such. Instead they hold Seer-un-Nabi meetings where speeches are made on different aspects of the life of this benefactor of mankind.

Guru Ram Das (S)

Guru Ram Das was born on September 24 1534 in Chuna Mandi, Lahore. Being the first son of the family, he was called Jetha. His father Hari Das, who belonged to the Sodhi caste, was a petty trader, and even as a child Jetha had to supplement his income by selling boiled grams (black chick peas).

He lost his mother at an early age, and when seven lost his father too. His maternal grandmother took him away to live with her, where he had to spend his days in poverty. When he was twelve, his grandmother decided to leave her village and move to Goindwal, a city founded by Guru Amar Das (the third guru) on the banks of the River Beas, and they settled there.

At Goindwal, Ram Das began to live a life dedicated to the Guru's cause and would do any job for the Guru. He was privileged to meet Guru Angad Dev, the second Guru. He learnt the science of music and acquired mastery over the art of poetry and mythology and of the sacred compositions of the gurus.

In 1552 Guru Angad Dev passed on his apostolate to Amar Das, and in 1553, struck by the manifold qualities of Ram Das, Guru Amar Das decided to give the hand of his daughter Bibi Bhani to him in marriage. He stayed with his father-in-law and was closely associated with his ministry.

He commanded the full confidence of the Guru, and for this reason he deputised for the Guru in the court of King Akbar and accompanied him on a long journey to Hardwar to acquaint the people with his religion. Guru Amar Das was so impressed by him that in 1574 he got down from his seat, seated Jetha there, and placed five paisas and one coconut before him as a mark of handling over the Gur Guddi to him.

King Akbar had been very much impressed by the hallowed personality of Guru Ram Das and granted a certain portion of land, with a small pool, to him. He liked the place, and having invited craftsmen and traders there, he eventually founded Amritsar, a great trading centre as well as a place of worship. Amritsar is the religious capital of Sikhs. The city, in the course of time, grew to be the biggest centre of trade in Punjab. Laying the foundation of the city Ram Das Pur, which is now called Amritsar, was the most notable achievement of the guruship of Guru Ram Das.

Guru Ram Das also composed the Sikh wedding hymns, which now form a very important part of the Sikh marriage service.

Karva Chauth (H)

According to legend, a princess observed a fast for a whole day. When she broke the fast at dusk, she received news about her husband's death. As she made her way to her husband's dead body, Parvati, the consort of the Lord Siva, met her and blessed her. She gave the princess some blood out of her finger with which she was asked to anoint her dead husband. The man immediately sprang to life. Hence, on this day, married women observe a fast for the whole day, for the welfare, prosperity and longevity of their husbands.

Prayers are offered to the god Siva and his consort, Parvati. At dusk upon sighting the moon, water and flowers are offered to the household deity. An elderly woman usually recites the story of Karva Chauth and the fast is broken.

On this occasion, mothers bless their married daughters and present them with jewellery, garments and sweet-meats.

Hallow'een (C)

An ancient Celtic celebration which is a mixture of pagan ideas, folklore and religion, celebrating the end of the Celtic year. Witches and evil spirits have to be driven away before the beginning of the new year. Bonfires and the ceremonial extinguishing of fire and lights symbolise the end of the year. Many games and superstitions are associated with it.

All Souls' Day (C)

This festival has been kept for nearly one thousand years. A shipwrecked pilgrim was told by a hermit that the souls of the dead who had not yet gone to heaven were crying out because people were not praying enough for them. The pilgrim told Odila, Abbot of Cluny, who set aside the date before All Saints' Day as All Souls' Day. Christians pray for the souls of the dead and often take flowers to the family grave.

November
All Saints' Day (All Hall) (C)

This festival celebrates Christian saints known and unknown. Although it was originally held in May, its date is November 1 probably stems from Gregory III (died 741) who dedicated a chapel to 'All Saints' at St Peter's basilica on that day, and Gregory IV (died 844) ordered its universal observation. In the Eastern Church it is still kept on the first Sunday after Whitsun. It is a Roman Catholic Holy Day of Obligation; Roman Catholics are expected to attend church.

Guy Fawkes' Day (GB)

Guy Fawkes' Day is celebrated all over Britain on November 5. On this day in 1605, a conspirator called Guy Fawkes tried to blow up King James 1 of England and his Parliament.

The nationwide celebrations feature fireworks and bonfires on which effigies of Guy Fawkes are burnt. These effigies are usually made by children who beg passers-by on the streets for 'a penny for the guy'.

Since the abortive plot of 1605, the vaults of the House of Lords are always searched by the sovereign's bodyguard – the Yeoman of the Guard – before the state opening of Parliament.

Diwali – (Deepawali) (H)

Diwali is the corruption of the Sanskrit word 'Deepawali' meaning row or cluster of lights. The festival of lights, observed annually in honour of the goddess Lakshmi, is celebrated throughout the country with great rejoicing in the month of Karthika (October–November). Every Hindu, whether rich or poor, celebrates this festival.

Several legends are associated with the festival. Some celebrate it as Rama's victory over Ravana of Lanka and his safe return from exile to his capital, Ayodhya.

According to another legend, Diwali marks the coronation of King Vikramaditya, the king whose coronation is said to mark the Vikram Era, which is 48 years older than the Christian Era.

This festival is doubly important for the wealthy mercantile communities of western India. Diwali day marks the beginning of the New Year. Lakshmi – the goddess of wealth – is worshipped on this day and the merchants open new account books and start everything afresh.

Diwali is generally celebrated on two days. The government of India however has declared the first day as the official public holiday.

Sikh Diwali (S)

The Sikhs celebrate Diwali in honour of the sixth guru, Guru Hargobind. He was the son of Guru Arjan, the fifth Guru. Guru Hargobind became the sixth guru after his father was assassinated by the Mughals for refusing to change his faith in 1606.

Guru Hargobind was only eleven at that time. He decided to defend himself and his people by wearing the two swords of 'miri' and 'piri' – symbols of political and religious leadership. He also refused to pay the fine imposed on his father for preaching his religion.

On these grounds the officers of the Mughal Emperor Jehangir imprisoned him at the fort of Gwalior where he stayed in prison for about five years. Eventually, Jehangir examined the case personally and ordered the Guru's release.

Sharing his prison were 52 Hindu princes, who were not offered their liberty. Guru Hargobind said that he would only accept his release if the princes were also allowed to leave the prison with him. The reply of the prison officers was that as many princes as could pass through the narrow passage of the prison, holding on to the Guru's clothes, could go free.

The Guru ordered a cloak to be made which had long tassel-like ends. All the princes walked to freedom holding on to his train. That is why the Sikhs call Guru Hargobind 'Bandi-Chor' – the releaser of prisoners.

When the Guru returned to Amritsar in 1620, the Sikhs illuminated the Golden Temple in honour of his release. Thus Diwali has a special meaning. It symbolises freedom of conscience, freedom to practise one's own faith, to respect another person's faith and to fight persecution. Later, his grandson Guru Gobind Singh said, 'There is only one race – the human race.' Everybody is invited to share in the celebrations.

On Diwali day, Sikhs from far and wide gather in the precincts of the Golden Temple from early morning. At night the temple and the surrounding buildings are illuminated with candles, lamps and electric bulbs.

The reflections of illuminations in the pool surrounding the Golden Temple add to the beauty and grandeur of the temple. There are also firework displays. Treasures accumulated during the Sikh rule are put on show and a general gala atmosphere pervades the town. In Britain, too, people decorate their homes and use candles and light bulbs to illuminate them. Sweets and presents are exchanged. People go to worship at the Gurdwaras and other holy places, which are specially decorated for the occasion.

Succession of Guru Granth Sahib (S)

It is said that three days before his passing away, Guru Gobind Singh finished the human succession to guruship and installed the 'Adi Granth' as Sri Guru Granth Sahib in 1708. The word guru means a guide or a teacher, a dispeller of the darkness of ignorance by sharing the light of spiritual knowledge with the world. The 1430 page Holy Book contains writings of the gurus and Hindu and Muslim saints, thereby making it a universal book of prayer. It occupies the central place in a Sikh Gurudwara.

The Birthday of Baha'u'llah (B)

He was born before sunrise, in the year 1817, of a wealthy family, and his father was a Minister of State at the court of Shah. Upon his death when his son was 22 years old, his post was offered to the young man, who turned it down, and the Prime Minister said, 'but I am convinced that he is destined for some lofty career. . . .'. He accepted the mission of the Bab and accordingly suffered the fate of thousands of those who thought as he did, and was imprisoned under awful conditions. However, it was in the dungeon that he experienced his revelation.

His birthday is celebrated with parties as well as the community gathering. Gifts are given, and cards sent to absent friends overseas.

Guru Nanak's Birthday (S)

Guru Nanak was born in the fifteenth century in the plains of the Punjab. He was born on October 20, 1469 (April 15 according to some scholars) in Rai Bhoe ki Talwandi, now known as Nankana Sahib in the Sheikupur district of west Pakistan. His father, Mehta Kalu, was a patwari, fairly high in the revenue department. His mother's name was Tripta and he had an elder sister named Nanki, four years his senior.

Guru Nanak was the founder of the Sikh religion and the first guru of the Sikhs. He was followed by nine successive gurus.

When he was five years old like many other children he was sent to an elementary school. He also attended Brij Nath's school for two years and was introduced to vedas (ancient scriptures) and philosophy. He was then sent to a Mohammedan teacher to learn Persian and Arabic to get a good post in a department of the government. He made himself familiar with the popular creeds both of the Mohammedans and the Hindus and he gained a general knowledge of the Quran and the brahmanical shastras. He displayed a remarkable grasp of vedic upanishadics (philosophical dispositions), Quranic, Arabic and other philosophical literature.

At nine he was required by custom to invest himself with the sacred thread 'Janaeu', as the Hindus call it, but he refused to do so, saying that he would rather have a thread that would neither break nor get soiled nor be burnt or lost. (The ceremony of investing with the sacred thread is, strictly speaking, a Brahmin custom of confirmation in which a cotton chord is placed on an 8 to 10 year old male. It is worn over the shoulder and across the chest. The twisted cotton thread is slightly thinner than a pencil). The Guru's view of the custom was:

'Out of the cotton of compassion spin the thread of contentment Tie ends of continence, give it the twist of truth. Make such a sacred thread for the mind. Such a thread once worn will never break nor get soiled burnt or lost. The man who weareth such a thread is blessed.'

His mind was so fixed on God that for some time he would do nothing but sing his praise and meditate on his name. In order to take him out of this mood, his father tried him in various professions, but failed. At last he put him to a trade. He was sent to a neighbouring town with 20 Rupees to buy goods of common use and sell them at a profit. On the way he came across a group of faqirs (saints) who had been hungry for several days. Guru Nanak spent the money in feeding them. He considered it to be a profitable business or sacha sauda (true bargain). His father flew into a rage and gave him a slap. It did not affect him at all and he passed more and more time in meditation.

At the age of sixteen, he married and had two sons. Even the responsibility of marriage and a family could not make him worldly-wise. At last he was sent to Sultanpur to his sister and was put in charge of the state granary. His inward struggle reached a crisis when a charge was labelled against him that he was recklessly giving away the grain. An inquiry was conducted, accounts were scrutinised and grain was re-weighed. It showed a balance in favour of the Guru. He sent in his resignation and decided to spread his message.

The first utterance of Nanak as Gur was that there is no Hindu and no Mussal man. He required a Hindu to be a good Hindu and a Muslim to be a good Muslim. He wanted the man to be a good human being and preached the concept of One God (Ek Onkar).

He synthesised the Hindu and Islamic systems into a new faith. His message was simple. He accepted the universal brotherhood under the fatherhood of God. He laid stress on the performance of duty. One must work for the good of all, and all must work and secure the good of each member of the society. He sought to bring man back to the path of true and purified religion.

To spread his message he undertook ardous and extensive tours in the north, south, east and west and visited the important centres of Hindus, Muslims, Buddhists, Jains, Sufis, Jogis and other religions and met people of different races, tribes and diverse cultural patterns.

Guru Nanak's life can be divided into three periods on the basis of his activities. The first period covers his childhood and early manhood, mostly spent in meditation; the second period was spent in travelling; and last period was that of relatively settled life at Kartarpur where he lived the life of an ordinary farmer.

He established a network of centres which he called 'Msulis' side-by-side with the centres of all other faiths. The community of inspired disciples became the body of the Sikh Church which he called 'Sangat'. He established a Sikh Church all over India, and outside India in Ceylon, Tibet and the Middle East. He made it clear to everyone that his Church was to be embedded in secular society.

He added emphasis to the religious and social discipline as well. The Japji, Rehras and Kirtan Sohila were fixed as morning, evening and night prayers. He himself worked in his fields, and his disciples were advised and encouraged to have regular daily labour, have normal relationships with their families and give some of their income to a good cause.

He also laid the foundation of the regular free kitchen. Everyone worked for his living and gave a part of his earnings for the free community kitchen. All the people, Muslim or Hindu, king or pauper, brahmin or low caste, had to sit together and eat their meals. His birthday is one of the most important festivals of the Sikh calendar.

Day of the Covenant (B)

An anniversary, not a holy day. When Baba'u'llah died, He left a will and testament decreeing that the believers should turn to his eldest son, whom he referred to as the 'Most Great Branch, the 'Branch from the Ancient Root', and 'The Master', and the Centre of His Covenant. It ensured that there should be no divergence of opinion among the believers, and no split in the community, as all turned to Abdu'l-Baha for guidance. In his turn, Abdu'l-Baha appointed his eldest grandson to be the sole interpreter of his words and those of Baha'u'llah, and the Guardian, as he was called, left provision for the election of the Universal House of Justice, which Abdu'l-Baha had outlined and said, 'Whatever they say is of God. Whoever obeys them has obeyed God, and whoever has disobeyed them has disobeyed God'. Abdu'l-Baha is known as the Centre of the Covenant, and as the perfect exemplar of the faith.

Ascension of Abdu'l-Baha (B)

In 1921, in Haifa, Israel (then Palestine) Abdu'l-Baha suffered years of imprisonment, before being set free by the Young Turks Rising, after which he travelled to the West, including Britain, where he met with many important people who flocked to see him and discuss various problems with him. At home in Palestine he was known as the 'father of the poor'. He was knighted by the British Government for saving the people from famine during the First World War, by having saved up grain in anticipation of such an event. Many thousands of mourners came together for his funeral, representing all levels of society, including the High Commissioner, Sir Herbert Samuel; the Governor of Jerusalem, the Consuls of various countries, the heads of the various religious communities, Jews, Christians, Moslems, Druzes, Egyptians, Greeks. The representatives of the Jews, Christians and Moslems raised their voices in eulogy and regret. 'So united were they in their acclamation of him as the wise educator and reconciler of the human race in this perplexed and sorrowful age, that there seemed to be nothing left for the Baha'is to say' – Lady Blomfield. His funeral was truly the uniting of many peoples of all races, creeds and colours. He was interred in the shrine on Mount Carmel. The believers commemorate the event at about 1.30 am.

St Andrew's Day (C)

St Andrew is the patron saint of Scotland. Andrew was a disciple of Jesus and the brother of Peter. Not much is known about him, except that traditionally he was crucified on an X-shaped cross and that in the thirteenth century some monks brought his relics to Scotland to secure their own protection.

In the Anglican Church the day is used to make intercessions for foreign missions.

December
First Day of Chanucah (Jw)

This festival commemorates the heroic efforts of the Maccabean brothers to lead the war to oust the Syrian/Greek invaders, who not only ruled Israel at the time but also passed laws proscribing the practice of Judaism, and desecrated the Temple by offering sacrifices in it of unclean animals.

When in 165, before the Common Era, the Syrians were defeated, the Maccabeans made their way to the Temple, cleansed it, reconsecrated it, and re-lit the Menorah, the light of which signified God's presence.

Miraculously, the special oil which was found and which should have lasted for only one day, was found to be enough for eight days, giving the priests enough time to obtain a new consignment of oil.

In commemoration of these events, candles or oil lamps are lit for eight days in Jewish homes.

Jewish children may attend school on these days.

Enlightenment of the Buddha (B)

In Zen temples, there is a period of intense meditation which re-enacts the Buddha's striving for enlightenment.

Feast of the Immaculate Conception (C)

Popular early Christian devotion to the Virgin Mary was confirmed at the Council of Ephesus in 431 when she was proclaimed to be the Mother of God. In subsequent centuries Christians, both Eastern and Western, advanced and extended devotion to the Virgin Mary. In honour of her special position in the history of mankind's redemption, the redemptive effects of the life, death and resurrection of Jesus were anticipated at her birth. In 1854 Pope Pius IX declared that Mary as the Immaculate Conception was conceived free from original sin.

Four years after the declaration of Pius IX, a young French girl, Bernadette Soubirous, had a vision of Mary at Lourdes. In the apparition Mary introduced herself as the 'Immaculate Conception'. Since then Catholics from all over the world have flocked to Lourdes in pilgrimage. Pilgrims find that the great chorus of hymns, the torch light processions and the rows of hopeful sick create a deep sense of pilgrimage.

Martyrdom of Guru Tegh Bahadur (S) (1621–1675)

Guru Tegh Bahadur was the ninth guru of the Sikhs and the son of Guru Hargobind, the sixth guru. He toured the whole of Punjab, Delhi, eastern India and Assam preaching the message of the fatherhood of God and the brotherhood of man, as it was preached by Guru Nanak. The Mughal ruler of the time was Aurangzeb who was actively using the machinery of state to quicken the process of Islamisation amongst his subjects, who were mainly Hindus. Many Hindu schools were closed, temples demolished, and mosques built on the sites. Taxes were imposed on non-Muslims when visiting their own holy places, and Jasia, another tax, was imposed on all non-Muslims. Those who could not pay were forcibly converted.

The story goes that a group of Hindu brahmins (priests) came from Kashmir with the news that the ruler of that place was forcibly converting people by breaking their sacred threads and wiping their marks off their foreheads – two important signs of a high-caste Hindu. They said that they had heard about Guru Tegh Bahadur as their only saviour and had come to seek his help.

When the Guru heard this tale of oppression, he is said to have remarked that this situation could only be relieved through the sacrifice of a holy person. His nine-year-old son, Gobind Rai, who later became the tenth guru, remarked, 'Who is holier than you to make this sacrifice, father?' At this point, Guru Tegh Bahadur told the Kashmiri brahmins to go back to their place and tell the ruler that they would change their faith only if Guru Tegh Bahadur became a convert.

Guru Tegh Bahadur's martyrdom is seen by the Sikhs not only as the act of a man accepting death for his own beliefs but also on behalf of another religion and for the promotion of religious liberty as a principle. Guru Gobind Singh composed these verses about his father's sacrifice.

'To preserve their caste marks and sacred threads,
Did he in the dark age, perform the supreme sacrifice,
He went to the utmost limit to help the saintly,
He gave his head but never cried in pain.'

The Sikhs have now built a Gurudwara at the place of execution. This martyrdom day is celebrated with great enthusiasm in Delhi, with a procession taking place one day before the event. Celebrations are held in the Gurudwaras wherever the Sikhs are, on the actual day in India, or on the nearest Sunday in the West. They consist of hymn singing, discourses, lectures and sacred food.

Christmas Eve (C)

On Christmas Eve carol services and midnight masses are held at churches and cathedrals throughout the world to celebrate the birth of Christ.

Christmas Day (C)

This festival celebrates the birth of Christ. Although it is likely that Jesus was born at a different time of the year, December 25 was probably used to coincide and change the Roman festival of the birthday of the unconquered sun. (December 21 is now the shortest day of the year due to a calendar correction in 1752.)

The first Christians did not keep Christmas, but by the fourth century, it was celebrated.

January 6, which was used a lot in the East, was originally used for a commemoration of a heresy that 'divine Christ appeared' only at his baptism by John. The Eastern Church still uses Epiphany (or appearing) whereas the Western Church adopted December 25 because Rome did between 336 and 353.

Although our calendar dates from Christ's birth, there have been miscalculations. Jesus was born when Herod was king and the Romans were ruling, and Herod died in what we refer to as 4 BC. The Roman calendar was used when Jesus was born and continued to be used until the sixth century. In AD 533, a Russian monk named Dionysius made the Christian calendar but miscalculated. It is reckoned Jesus was born sometime between 7 BC and 4 BC.

Christmas is celebrated with joy and merry-making. Friends and families get together and give presents, remembering the gift of Christ and the gifts given to Jesus. Peace and good will to all men is proclaimed in the singing of Christmas carols. Often candelight services are held.

Christmas Customs

Many of the modern Christmas customs are directly derived from ceremonies associated with ancient mid-winter feasts. One of the oldest is probably the decoration of houses and churches with greenery. Evergreens – the symbol of everlasting life – were commonly used to decorate dwellings and sacred buildings in ancient times at the time of the winter solstice, and the custom has endured despite the efforts of the early Christian Church to put an end to the practice.

Holly and ivy were the favourite plants, although laurel was also used. Mistletoe, sacred to the Druids, was used in houses but it was and still is banned from some churches. The custom of kissing under the mistletoe is entirely English in origin.

The Christmas tree is a relative newcomer to England. It came originally from Germany, and went to America with the German settlers before it reached the British Isles some-where in the early nineteenth century. The first English Christmas tree of which there is any clear record was one set up at a children's party by a member of Queen Caroline's Court in 1821. The custom of having a Christmas tree as an important symbol of the festival, however, became widespread only after Prince Albert, the Consort of Queen Victoria, set one up at Windsor Castle in 1841.

Since 1947, the Norwegian capital, Oslo, has made an annual gift of an immense Christmas tree to the people of London. This stands brightly lit, in Trafalgar Square, close to Nelson's Monument.

Many churches now have a Christmas crib, although not so long ago these were rarely seen except in Roman Catholic churches and homes. Tradition says it was St Francis of Assisi who made the first crib in 1224.

Exchanging presents and Christmas cards are essential features of the Christmas festival, though the custom has its roots in pre-Christian times. Presents were given to the poor and to relatives at the feast of the Saturnalia in ancient Rome. The Christmas card began its existence as the 'Christmas piece' – a decorated sheet of paper on which school children wrote polite greetings for the season in their best handwriting and presented these to their parents.

Father Christmas is the traditional bearer of gifts in Britain. Originally he was more the personification of the joys of Christmas than a gift-giver. He is mentioned in a fifteenth-century carol which began, 'Hail, Father Christmas, hail to thee!' and has been a familiar figure for centuries. Parliament abolished him in 1644 but he came back after the Restoration. In the nineteenth century he acquired some of the attributes of the Teutonic Santa Klaus and now children think of him as the bearer of gifts, coming at night from the North Pole in his reindeer-drawn sleigh and entering homes through the chimneys.

The Yule log was one of the main features of Christmas festivities in England and other European countries. The traditional log was usually of oak or ash and as large as the widest fireplace in the house would allow. It was brought in on Christmas Eve with great ceremony and rejoicing and lit with a fragment of its predecessor of the year before. It had to burn steadily throughout the twelve days of Christmas and at the end was put out, and a portion was saved to use in kindling the next year's log so that there would be a continuity of good fortune and blessing. It was never allowed to burn away completely.

Christmas food has been largely a matter of tradition. Turkey, the most usual dish on Christmas day, did not appear in Britain until about 1542 and was not very popular until much later. Its predecessors were goose and pork, or a huge Christmas pie made from a variety of birds. In richer houses, venison, swans or peacocks were eaten. However, the boar's head was always considered to be the most succulent dish of all. It was usually brought to the table on a gold or silver platter and with great ceremony.

The ancestor of the modern Christmas pudding was plum porridge – a mixture of meat broth, raisins, spices, fruit and wine. When puddings are made at home, every member of the family is expected to make a wish while waiting their turn to stir it. A few small charms such as a silver coin (promising wealth), a ring (promising speedy marriage) and a thimble (prophesying a single life) are included in the mixture.

The tradition of eating mince pies is older than plum pudding as they were already well known by the end of the sixteenth century. They were originally more varied in content, including items such as chopped chicken, eggs, spices and raisins, all contained in little pastry cases known as 'coffins'. According to tradition, one should be eaten on each of the twelve days of Christmas to ensure twelve happy months in the coming year.

In England, the traditional Christmas drink was the wassail which was always served in a large brown vessel made of apple wood. It consisted of ale, roast apples, eggs, sugar, nutmegs, cloves and ginger and was drunk while hot.

Wassail comes from two old Saxon words, 'was haile' meaning 'your health'. In Victorian times, the wassail bowl was carried from door to door in rural areas. Neighbours would fill the bowl with ale or cider to ensure a good apple harvest the next autumn.

Carols were never considered to be religious hymns. Rather, they were the popular songs of the Christian religion which came into being after the religious revival of the thirteenth century. Puritanism swept away the English carols and they did not come back into general favour for nearly 200 years. Now, nearly all churches have a carol service and groups of children go from home to home, singing carols and being rewarded with mince pies and money.

December 26 is the feast of St Stephen, the first Christian martyr. In England, this anniversary is popularly known as Boxing Day. The name is thought to be derived later from the alms boxes in churches which were opened on this day and their contents distributed amongst the poor, or else from the earthernware boxes apprentices carried when they were collecting gifts of money from their master's customers. Until recently it was usual for the postman, dustman and other public employees to call at the houses they served to receive small gifts.

For over 800 years, one of the regular Christmas entertainments was mumming, when young men and women dressed up, sometimes in each others clothes, wore masks and gave a display of dancing or enacted a play at the homes of the rich people. They were usually rewarded with a gift of money or food.

In the course of time, the dialogue and action underwent several changes, although the central theme continued to be the victory of good over evil. At the end of play, there was usually some clowning and gaiety in which all the characters would join.

Plays about the nativity were part of miracle plays, which became popular between the thirteenth century and sixteenth century. They were based on Bible stories and were originally performed as part of a church service.

The Reformation checked the popularity of miracle plays and gave rise to the morality play, which was mainly concerned with the behaviour of men and women.

Pantomime is an entirely British form of entertainment. It is believed to have originated in the eighteenth century and continues to be a popular feature of Christmas festivities and celebrations.

Thai New Year (Th)

See April, Sonkrar Day. (page 34)

Guru Gobind Singh (S)

Guru Gobind Singh was the tenth guru of the Sikhs. He was born at Patna in the Bihar state of India on December 22, 1666. The language of the area had a great impact on his poetry, though he studied not only the Bihari language but also Sanskrit, Persian and Arabic.

As a child he used to have mock battles with other children on the bank of Ganges and was noted as a great marksman whose arrows never missed the target. At the age of seven he went to Anandpur in Punjab where the arrangements were made for his further studies of languages. He also learnt archery and swordsmanship.

He became Guru at the age of nine years after the martyrdom of Guru Tegh Bahadur, and began to consolidate his position as the spiritual head of the community. He lived at Paonta on the banks of the Yamna from 1682 to 1686 and engaged himself in literary pursuits. Several Sanskrit and Persian classics were translated into Brij Bhasha. He had 52 court poets, and most of them helped in the translations. He himself wrote a lot of poetry which is compiled in Dasam Granth.

On Baisakhi day of 1699 he established the Sikh brotherhood and Khalsa was born when five beloved ones presented themselves at his command. He abolished the caste prejudice and treated women as equals. He gave the name Singh (lion) to men and Kaur (princess) to women. He revolutionised the passive resistance movement and gave the concept of Saint Soldier. He gave common worship, common place of pilgrimage, common baptism for all classes and common external appearance. By this he brought unity among his followers and gave the slogan 'The Khalsa is God, the victory is of God'.

On October 7, 1708, he called his followers, placed five paisas and a coconut before Guru Granth Sahib, the holy book, and bowed to it as his successor. He told the congregation to behold Guru Granth Sahib as the visible body of the Guru and read it for guidance in future. Guru Granth Sahib is the last guru of the Sikhs. Guru Gobind Singh's birthday is celebrated in the whole world wherever there is a Sikh community. His life story is told to the congregation and the hymns are sung in his memory.

1989 to 1993 Calendars

KEY

B	=	Bahai
Bd	=	Buddhist
C	=	Christian
Ch	=	Chinese
H	=	Hindu
J	=	Japanese
Jw	=	Jewish
M	=	Moslem
Sc	=	Secular
S	=	Sikh
SL	=	Sri Lanka
T	=	Tibetan
Th	=	Thai

1989

January	February	March
1.....New Year's Day (C)	St Brigid's Day (C)	St David's Day (C)
1.....Ganjitsu New Year Japan (J)		
2	Candlemas (C)	
3	Setsubun (J)	Hina Matsuri (J)
4		
5		Shab-I-Miraj (M)
6.....Epiphany (C)	New Year (Snake) (Ch)	
6.....Serbian Christmas (O)		
7	7–9 Losar (T)	Shivratri (H)
7	Shrove Tuesday (C)	
8	Ash Wednesday (C)	
8	Lent (C)	
9		
10	Basant Panchami (H)	
11		
12.....Lohri (S)		
13.....Makar Sankranti (H)		
14.....Bhogi Pongal (H)		
14.....Guru Gobind Singh's Birthday (S)		
15.....Mathu Pongal (H)		
16		
17		St Patrick's Day (C)
18–25 Christian Unity Week (C)		
19		Palm Sunday (C)
20	Maghapuja (Bd)	
21.....Tu B'Shevat (Jw)		Baha'i New Year 145 (B)
21		Purim (Jw)
21		Higan (Bd)
22		Holi (H)
23		Holla Mohalla (H)
24		Shab-I-Bharat (M)

25 ....

26 ....Easter Sunday (C) ....

27 ....

28 ....

29 ....

30 ....

31 ....

1989

April	May	June
1 .....April Fool's Day (SC)	May Day(C)	
2	Twelfth Day of Ridvan (B)	
2	Lailat-ul-Qadr (M)	
2	Yom Hashoah (Jw)	
3	Kodomo no Hi (J)	
3	Juma-Tul-Wida (M)	
4–6 Qingming (Ch)	Ascension Day (C)	
5		
6 .....Ramadhan (M)	Eid-ul-Fitr (M)	
7		
8		Dragon Boat Festival (Ch) ....
9		Shavout (Jw)................................
10	Yom Ha'atzmaut (Jw)	
11		
12		
13 ....Baisakhi (S)		
13 ....Sinhala and Tamil New Year (SL)		
14 .....or 15 Vishu (H)	Pentecost (C)	
14 ....Malyalam & Bengali New Year (H)		
14 ....Ramanavami (H)		
15	15–20 Christian Aid Week (C)	
16		
17		

18 ....

19 ....Vaisakhapuja (Bd) ....

20–27 Passover (Jw) ....

21 .....First Day of Ridvan (B) ....

22 ....

23 .....St George's Day (C) ....Declaration of the Bab (B)...................................

23 .....Maundy Thursday (C) ....

23 ....Lag B'Omer (Jw) ....

24 .....Good Friday (C) ....Corpus Christi (C) ....

25 .....Holy Saturday (C) ....

26 ....

27 ....

28 ....

29 .....Ninth Day of Ridvan (B) ....Ascension of Baha'u'llah (B) ....St Peter and St Paul (C)...........................

30 ....

31 ....

1989

July	August	September

1 ....

2 ....

3 ....Hijrat (Muslim New Year) ....

4 ....

5 ....

6 ....

7 ....

8 ....Onam (H) ....

9 .....Martyrdom of the Bab (B)...

10 ....Tish B'av (Jw) ....

11 ....

12 ....Ashuraa 10th Muharram (M) ....

13 .....Haj (M) ....

14 .....Eid-ul-Adha (M) ....

15 ....Mid-Autumn Festival (Ch) ....

16 ....

17 .....Asalhapuja (Bd).......................................Raksha Bandhan (H) ....

18 ....

19 ....

20 ....

21 ....

22 ....

23 ....Janmashtami (H) ....

24 ....

25 ....

26 ....

27 ....

28 ....

29 ....

30 ....New Year (Jw) ....

31 ....

1989

October	November	December

1 ....All Saints' Day (C)...

2 ....

3 ....

4 ....

5 ....Guy Fawkes' Day (GB)..

6 ....

7 ....

8 .....Chong Yang (Ch)..Feast of Immaculate Conception (C)

9 .....Yom Kippur (Jw)...

10 .....Dussehra (H) ....

11 ....

12 .....Eid Milad-un-Nabi (M) ....Birthday of Baha'u'llah (B) ....

13 ....Guru Nanak's Birthday (S)..

14 .....Succott (Tabernacles) (Jw)..

15 ....

16 ....

17 .....Karva Chauth (H)..

18 ....

19 ....

20 .....Birthday of the Bab (B)..

21 ....

22 .....Simchath Torah (Jw)...

23 ....

24 ....

25 ....Christmas Day (C).................................

26 ....Day of Covenant (B)......................St Stephen's Day (C)................................

26 ....Boxing Day (C)...

27 ....

28 ....Ascension of Abdu'l-Baha (B)..

29 .....Diwali (H) ....

30 ....St Andrew's Day (C)..

31 .....All Souls' Day (C)...

1990

January	February	March
1 .....New Year's Day (C)	St Brigid's Day (C)	St David's Day (C)
1 .....Ganjitsu New Year Japan (J)		
2	Candlemas (C)	
3 .....Guru Gobind Birthday (S)	Setsubun (J)	Hina Matsuri (J)
4		
5		
6 .....Epiphany (C)		
6 .....Serbian Christmas (O)		
7		
8		
9	Maghapuja (Bd)	
10	Basant Panchami (H)	
10	Tu B'Shevat (Jw)	
11		Purim (Jw)
12		
13 .....Lohri (S)		
14 .....Makar Sankranti (H)		
14 .....Bhogi Pongal (H)	Shab-I-Bharat (M)	
15 .....Mathu Pongal (H)		
16		
17		St Patrick's Day (C)
18–25 Christian Unity Week (C)		
19		
20		
21		Baha'i New Year 146 (B)
22		Holi (H)
23		Lailat-ul-Qadr (M)
23		Holla Mohalla (H)
24	Shivratri (H)	
25	Shar-I-Miraj (M)	Mothering Sunday (C)
26	26–28 Losar (T)	

27.....New Year (Horse) (Ch) ....Shrove Tuesday (C) ....

28 ....Ash Wednesday (C).............................Ramadhan (M) ....

28 ....Lent (C) ....

29 ....

30 ....

31 ....

1990

April	May	June

1 .....April Fool's Day (SC) ....May Day (C)..

2 ....Twelfth Day of Ridvan (B) ....

3 .....Ramanavami (H) ....Pentecost (C)...

4–6 Qingming (Ch) ....

5 ....Kodomo no Hi (J)..

6 ....

7 ....

8 .....Palm Sunday (C) ....Vaisakhapuja (Bd) ....

9 ....

10–17 Passover (Jw)...

11 ....

12 .....Maundy Thursday (C) ....

13 .....Sinhala and Tamil New Year Day (SL) Lag B'Omer (Jw) ....

13 .....Baisakhi (S)..

13 .....Good Friday (C) ....

14 .....Vishu (H)..14–19 Christian Aid Week (C)..................Corpus Christi (C) ....

14 .....Malyalam and Bengali New Year (H) ....

14 .....Holy Saturday (C)..

15 ....

16 ....

17 ....

18 ....

19 ....

20 ....

21 .....First Day of Ridvan (B) ....
22 .....Yom Hashoah (Jw) ....Declaration of the Bab (B) ....
23 ....
24 .....Juma-Tul-Wida (M) ....Ascension Day (C) ....
25 ....
26 .....Eid-ul-Fitr (M) ....
27 ....
28 ....Dragon Boat Festival (Ch) ....
29 .....Ninth Day of Ridvan (B) ....Ascension of Baha'u'llah (B) ....St Peter and St Paul (C)................................
30 .....Yom Ha'atzmaut (Jw) ....Shavout (Jw) ....
31 ....

1990

July	August	September

1 ....
2 ....Ashuraa 10th Muharram (M) ....
3 .....Haj (M) ....
4 .....Eid-Ul-Adha (M) ....
5 ....
6 ....Raksha Bandhan (H) ....
7 .....Asalhapuja (Bd) ....
8 ....
9 .....Martyrdom of the Bab (B) ....
10 ....
11 ....
12 ....
13 .....Janmashtami (H) ....
14 ....
15 ....
16 ....
17 ....
18 ....
19 ....

20 ....New Year (Jw) ....

21 ....

22 ....

23 ....

24 ....

25 .....Hijrat (Muslim New Year) ....Onam (H) ....

26 ....

27 ....

28 ....

29 ....Yom Kippur (Jw) ....

30 ....Harvest Festival (Ch) ....

31 .....Tish B'av (Jw) ....

1990

October	**November**	**December**

1 ....All Saints' Day (C) ....

2 .....Eid-Milad-un-Nabi (M)...........................Guru Nanak's Birthday (S) ....

3 ....

4 .....Mid-Autumn Festival (Ch) ....

4 .....Succott (Jw) ....

5 ....Guy Fawkes' Day (GB) ....

6 ....

7 .....Karva Chauth (H)...

8 ....Feast of Immaculate Conception (C)

9 ....

10 .....Dussehra (H) ....

11 ....

12 .....Simchath Torah (Jw)...........................Birthday of Baha'u'llah (B) ....Chanucah (Jw)...........................

13 ....

14 ....

15 ....

16 ....

17 ....

18.....Diwali (H)

19

20.....Birthday of the Bab (B)

21

22

23

24 ....Guru Gobind's Birthday (S)

25 ....Christmas Day (C)

26.....Chon Yang (Ch).....................................Day of Covenant (B)........................St Steven's Day (C)

26 ....Boxing Day (C)

27

28 ....Ascension of Abdu'l-Baha (B)

29

30 ....St Andrew's Day (C)

31.....All Souls' Day (C)

1991

January	February	March
1.....New Year's Day (C)	St Brigid's Day (C)	Hola Mohalla (S)
1.....Ganjitsu New Year Japan (J)		St David's Day (C)
2	Candlemas (C)	
3	Setsubun (J)	Hina Matsuri (J)
4		Shab-I-Bharat (M)
5		
6.....Epiphany (C)		
6.....Serbian Christmas (O)		
7		
8		
9		
10	Basant Panchami (H)	Mothering Sunday (C)
11		
12	Shrove Tuesday (C)	
13.....–Lohri (S)	Shivratri (H)	
13	Ash Wednesday (C)	Lailat-ul-Qadr (M)
13	Lent (C)	
14.....Makar Sankranti (H)		
14.....Bhogi Pongal (H)		
15.....Mathu Pongal (H)	Shab-I-Miraj (M)	
15	New Year Goat (Ch)	
16	15–17 Losar (T)	
17		St Patrick's Day (C)
18–25 Christian Unity Week (C)		Ramadhan (M)
19		
20		
21		Baha'i New Year 147 (B)
21		Higan (Bd)
22		
23		
24		Palm Sunday (C)

24	....	Ramanavami (H) ....
25		
26		
27		
28	Maghapuja (Bd)	Maundy Thursday (C)
28	Holi (H)	
28	Purim (Jw)	
29		Good Friday (C)
30	Tu B'Shevat (Jw)	30–6 Passover (Jw)
30		Holy Saturday (C)
31		Easter Sunday (C)

1991

April	May	June
1 ....April Fool's Day (SC)	May Day(C)	
2	Twelfth Day of Ridvan (B)	
2	Lag B'Omer (Jw)	
3		
3		
4–6 Qingming (Ch)		
5	Kodomo no Hi (J)	
6		
7		
8		
9	Ascension Day (C)	
10		
11		
12 ....Yom Hashoah (Jw)		
13 ....Sinhala and Tamil New Year's Day (SL)	13–18 Christian Aid Week (C)	
14 ....Baisakhi (S)		
14 ....Vishu (H)		
14 ....Malyalam and Bengali New Year (H)		

14.....Juma-Tul-Wida (M)..

15..

16...Dragon Boat Festival (Ch).............................

17.....Eid-Ul-Fitr (M)...

18.....Yom Ha'atzmaut (Jw)..

19..Pentecost (C) Shavout (Jw)...

20..

21.....First Day of Ridvan (B)...

22..

23.....St George's Day (C)..................................Declaration of the Bab (B)...

24...Haj (M)..

25...Eid-Ul-Adha (M)...

26..

27..

28...Vaisakhapuja (Bd)...

29.....Ninth Day of Ridvan (B)..........................Ascension of Baha'u'llah (B).................St Peter and St Paul (C)...........................

30...Corpus Christi (C)..

31..

1991

July	August	September
1..Janmashtami (H)...................................		
2..		
3..		
4..		
5..		
6..		
7..Onam (H)..		
8..		
9.....Martyrdom of the Bab (B)...New Year (Jw)................................		
10..		
11..		
12..		

13 ....

14 .....Hijrat (Muslim New Year) ....

15 ....

16 ....

17 ....

18 ....Yom Kippur (Jw)....................................

19 ....

20 ....

21 .....Tish B'av (Jw) ....

22 ....

23 ....Mid-Autumn Festival (Ch) ....

23 ....Succott (Jw)..

23 ....Eid Milad-un-Nabi (M) ....

24 .....Ashuraa 10th Muharram (M) ....

25 ....Raksha Bandhan (H) ....

26 .....Asalhapuja (Bd)..

27 ....

28 ....

29 ....Harvest Festival (C)..............................

30 ....

31 ....

1991

October	November	December
1 .....Simcath Torah (Jw)	All Saint's Day (C)......................................	
2	....	Chanucah (Jw)...................................
3		
4		
5	Guy Fawkes' Day (GB)............................	
5	Diwali (H)	
6		
7		
8		Feast of Immaculate Conception (C)

9 ....

10 ....

11 ....Birthday of Baha'u'llah (B)...

12 ....

13 ....

14 ....

15 ....

16 .....Chong Yang (Ch)...

17 .....Dussehra (H)...

18 ....

19 ....

20 .....Birthday of the Bab (B)...

21 ....Guru Nanak's Birthday (S)...

22 ....

23 ....

24 ....

25 ....Christmas Day (C)......................

26 .....Karva Chauth (H)......................................Day of Covenant (B)...............................St Stephen's Day (C) ....

26 ....Boxing Day (C)...........................

27 ....

28 ....Ascension of Abdu'l-Baha (B)...

29 ....

30 ....St Andrew's Day (C)..

31 .....All Souls' Day (C)..

1992

January	February	March
1.....New Year's Day (C)	St Brigid's Day (C)	St David's Day (C)
1.....Ganjitsu New Year's Day Japan (J)		
2	Candlemas (C)	
3	Setsubun (J)	Shrove Tuesday (C)
3		Lailat-ul-Qadr (M)
3		Hina Matsuri (J)
3		Shivratri (H)
4	New Year (Monkey) (Ch)	Ash Wednesday (C)
4		Lent (C)
5	Shab-I-Miraj (M)	5–7 Losar (T)
6.....Epiphany (C)		
6.....Serbian Christmas (O)		
7		
8		Ramadhan (M)
9	Basant Panchami (H)	
10		
11		
12.....Guru Gobind's Birthday (S)		
13.....Lohri (S)		
14.....Makar Sankranti (H)		
14.....Bhogi Pongal (H)		
15.....Mathu Pongal (H)		
16		St Patrick's Day (C)
17		
18–25 Christian Unity Week (C)	Maghapuja (Bd)	Holi (C)
19		Purim (Jw)
19		Hola Mohalla (S)
20.....Tu B'Shevat (Jw)		
21		Baha'i New Year 148 (B)
21		Higan (Bd) (J)
22		

23 ....

24 ....Shab-I-Bharat (M) ....

25 ....

26 ....

27 ....

28 ....

29 ....Mothering Sunday (C) ....

30 ....

31 ....

1992

April	May	June
1 ....April Fool's Day (SC)	May Day(C)	
2	Twelfth Day of Ridvan (B)	
3		
4–6 Qingming (Ch)		
4 ....Juma-tul-Wida (M)	Yom Ha'atzmaut (Jw)	
5	Kodomo no Hi (J)	Dragon Boat Festival (Ch)
6		
7 ....Eid-Ul-Fitr (M)		Pentecost (C)
7		Shavout (Jw)
8		
9		
10		
11 ....Ramanavami (H)	11–16 Christian Aid Week (C)	
12 ....Palm Sunday (C)		
13 ....Sinhala and Tamil New Year Day (SL)		
13 ....Baisakhi (S)		
14 .....Malyalam and Bengali New Year (H)		
14 ....Vishu (H)		Haj (M)
15		Eid-Ul-Adhan (M)
16 ....Maundy Thursday (C)	Vaisakhapuja (Bd)	
17 ....Good Friday (C)		

18–25 Passover (Jw)..Corpus Christi (C)...

18 .....Holy Saturday (C)...

19 .....Easter Sunday (C)...

20 ....

21 .....First Day of Ridvan (B)..Lag B'Omer (Jw)...

22 ....

23 .....St George's Day (C)...Declaration of the Bab (B)..

24 ....

25 ....

26 ....

27 ....

28 ....Ascension Day (C)..

29 .....Ninth Day of Ridvan (B).........................Ascension of Baha'u'llah (B)................St Peter and St Paul (C)...........................

30 .....Yom Hashoah (Jw)..

31 ....

1992

July	August	September
1		
2		
3		
4		
5 .....Hijrat (Muslim New Year)..		
6		
7		
8		
9 .....Martyrdom of the Bab (B)........................Tish B'av (Jw)..		
10		
11		
12 ....Mid-Autumn Festival (Ch).......................		
13 ....Raksha Bandhan (H).................................Eid Milad-Un-Nabi (M).......................		
14 .....Asalhapuja (Bd)..		
15 .....Ashuraa 10th Muharram (M)..		

16 ....

17 ....

18 ....

19 ....

20 ....

21 ....Janamashtmi (H)..

22 ....

23 ....

24 ....Onam (H)..

25 ....

26 ....

27 ....

28 ....New Year (Jw)...........................

29 ....

30 ....Harvest Festival (C).................

31 ....

1992

October	November	December

1 ....All Saints' Day (C)...........................

2 ....

3 ....

4 .....Chong Yang (Ch)..

5 .....Dussehra (H) ....Guy Fawkes' Day (GB)...........................

6 ....

7 .....Yom Kippur (Jw)...

8 ....Feast of Immaculate Conception (C)

9 ....

10 ....Guru Nanak's Birthday (S)...........................

11 ....

12 .....Succott (Tabernacles) (Jw)................Birthday of Baha'u'llah (B)...........................

13 ....

14 ....

15.....Karva Chauth (H) ....

16 ....

17 ....

18 ....

19 ....

20 .....Simhat Torah (Jw) ....

20 .....Birthday of the Bab (B) .... Chanucah (Jw) ....

21 ....

22 ....

23 ....

24 ....

25 .....Diwali (H) .... Christmas Day (C) ....

26 .... Day of Covenant (B) .... St Stephen's Day (C) ....

26 .... Boxing Day (C) ....

27 ....

28 .... Ascension of Abdu'l-Baha (B) ....

29 ....

30 .... St Andrew's Day (C) ....

31 .....All Souls' Day (C) .... Guru Gobind's Birthday (S) ....

1993

January	February	March
1.....New Year's Day (C)	St Brigid's Day (C)	St David's Day (C)
1.....Ganjitsu New Yr Japan (J)		
2	Candlemas (C)	
3	Setsubuns (J)	Hina Matsuri (J)
4		
5		
6.....Tu B'Shevat (Jw)		
6.....Epiphany (C)		
6.....Serbian Christmas (O)		
7		Maghapuja (Bd)
7		Purim (Jw)
8		Holi (H)
9		Hola Mohalla (S)
10		
11		
12.....Lohri (S)		
13.....Makar Sankranti (H)		
14.....Bhogi Pongal (H)	Shab-I-Bharat (M)	
15.....Mathu Pongal (H)		
16		
17		St Patrick's Day (C)
18–25 Christian Unity Week (C)		
19		
20	Shivratri (H)	
21		Mothering Sunday (C)
21		Higan (Bd) (J)
21		Bahai New Year 149 (B)
22	Lailat-ul-Qadr (M)	
22.....22–24 Losar (T)		
23.....New Year (Cock) (Ch)	Shrove Tuesday (C)	
24	Ash Wednesday (C)	

24 ....Lent (C) ....

25 ....

26 ....Juma-Tul-Wida (M)..

27 .....Shab-I-Miraj (M) ....Ramadhan (M) ....

28 .....Basant Panchami (H) ....

29 ....Eid-Ul-Fitr (M) ....

30 ....

31 ....

1993

April	May	June

1 .....Ramanavami (H) ....

1 .....April Fool's Day (SC) ....May Day(C) ....

2 ....Twelfth Day of Ridvan (B) ....

3 ....

4–6 Qingming (Ch) ....Haj (M)...

4 .....Palm Sunday (C) ....Visakhapuja (Bd)..

5 ....Kodomo no Hi (J) ....Eid-Ul-Adha (M) ....

6–13 Passover (Jw) ....

7 ....

8 .....Maundy Thursday (C) ....

9 .....Good Friday (C) ....Lag B'Omer (Jw) ....Corpus Christi (C) ....

10 .....Holy Saturday (C) ....

11 .....Easter Sunday (C) ....

12 ....

13 .....Sinhala and Tamil New Year's
      Day (SL) ....

13 .....Baisakhi (S)..

14 .....Vishu (H) ....

14 .....Malyalam and Bengali New Year (H) ....

15 ....

16 ....Shavout (Jw)..

17 ....17–22 Christian Aid Week (C)...

18.....Yom Hashoah (Jw)		
19		
20	Ascension Day (C)	
21.....First Day of Ridvan (B)		
22		
23.....St George's Day (C)	Declaration of the Bab (B)	
24		Dragon Boat Festival (Ch)
25		
26.....Yom Ha'atzmaut (Jw)		Hijrat (Muslim New Year)
27		
28		
29.....Ninth Day of Ridvan (B)	Ascension of Baha'u'llah (B)	St Peter and St Paul (C)
30	Pentecost (C)	
31	Eid-ul-Adha (M)	

1993

July	August	September
1		
2	Asalhapuja (Bd)	
2	Raksha Bandhan (H)	
3		Eid-Milad-Un-Nabi (M)
4.....Ashuraa 10th Muharram (M)		
5		
6		Onam (H)
7		
8		
9.....Martyrdom of the Bab (B)		
10	Jannmashtami (H)	
11		
12		
13		
14		
15		

16 ....New Year (Jw) ....

17 .....Tish B'Av (Jw) ....

18 ....

19 ....

20 ....

21 ....

22 ....

23 ....

24 ....

25 ....

26 ....Yom Kippur (Jw) ....

27 ....

28 ....

29 ....

30 ....Harvest Festival (C) ....

30 ....Succott (Jw) ....

31 ....

1993

October	November	December

1 .....Mid-Autumn Feast (Ch) ....All Saints Day (C) ....

2 ....

3 ....Karva Chauth (H) ....

4 ....

5 ....Guy Fawkes Day (GB) ....

6 ....

7 ....Feast of Immaculate Conception (C)...

8 .....Simchath Torah (Jw) ....

9 ....Chanucah (Jw) ....

10 ....

11 ....Birthday of Baha'u'llah (B) ....

12 ....

13 ....Diwali (H) ....

14 ....

15 ....

16 ....

17 ....

18 ....

19 ....

20 .....Birthday of the Bab (B)...

21 ....

22 ....

23 .....Chong Yang (Ch)...

24 .....Dussehra (H) ....

25 ....Christmas Day (C)..

26 ....Day of Covenant (B)......................St Stephen's Day (C) ....

26 ....Boxing Day (C)..................................

27 ....

28 ....Ascension of Abdu'l-Baha (B)..

29 ....Guru Nanak's Birthday (S)...

30 ....St Andrew's Day (C)...

31 .....All Souls' Day (C)...

Index

Key

B	=	Bahai
Bd	=	Buddhist
C	=	Christian
Ch	=	Chinese
H	=	Hindu
J	=	Japanese
Jw	=	Jewish
M	=	Moslem
Sc	=	Secular
S	=	Sikh
SL	=	Sri Lanka
T	=	Tibetan
Th	=	Thai